1 KINGS 12–22

The Kingdom Divides

John MacArthur

THOMAS NELSON
Since 1798

MacArthur Bible Studies

1 Kings 12–22: The Kingdom Divides

Published in Nashville, Tennessee, by Nelson Books, an imprint of Thomas Nelson. Nelson Books and Thomas Nelson are registered trademarks of HarperCollins Christian Publishing, Inc.

Originally published in association with the literary agency of Wolgemuth & Associates, Inc. Original layout, design, and writing assistance by Gregory C. Benoit Publishing, Old Mystic, CT.

"Unleashing God's Truth, One Verse at a Time®" is a trademark of Grace to You. All rights reserved.

Thomas Nelson titles may be purchased in bulk for educational, business, fundraising, or sales promotional use. For information, please e-mail SpecialMarkets@ThomasNelson.com.

All Scripture quotations are taken from *The New King James Version.* © 1982 by Thomas Nelson. Used by permission. All rights reserved.

Some material from the Introduction, "Keys to the Text" and "Exploring the Meaning" sections taken from *The MacArthur Bible Commentary,* John MacArthur, Copyright © 2005 Thomas Nelson Publishers.

ISBN 978–07180–3473–3

HB 05.21.2024

CONTENTS

INTRODUCTION

When Israel entered the Promised Land they were a nation united, first under the leadership of judges and prophets, and then under the leadership of kings. The Lord established the monarchies of Israel with the specific intention that the nation's kings should be shepherds of God's people. The kings were not to lord their power over the Israelites but to serve as examples of godliness and humility.

The monarchy got off to a rocky start with King Saul, but under the rule of King David the Israelites were able to subdue most of their enemies and bring a time of peace to the land. When David's son Solomon assumed the throne, the Lord granted his request for wisdom to rule the people, and the Israelites entered into a time of prosperity. It was during Solomon's rule that the first temple was built in Jerusalem to honor the Lord.

Sadly, this "golden age" in Israel's history did not last, for Solomon married many foreign women and made compromises that ultimately led him into pagan worship. As a result, the Lord would end up rejecting him as king and dividing the nation into two parts: Israel in the north and Judah in the south. In this study, we will see that most of the rulers of both kingdoms would end up being unfaithful shepherds. In spite of repeated confrontations from God's appointed prophets, by and large the story of Israel and Judah's kings is the story of compromise and corruption—all at the expense of God's people.

In these twelve studies, we will examine the reign of kings depicted in 1 Kings 12–22 and witness what led so many of them to make such bad choices. We will look at the foolishness of Rehoboam (under whose reign the kingdom divided), the up-and-down reign of Asa, and the rule of the notoriously wicked Ahab and Jezebel. We will also examine some of the individuals who stood against the idolatry and syncretism that polluted Israel—prophets such as Elijah, Obadiah, and Micaiah—who proclaimed God's truth at risk of their own lives.

Through it all, we will learn some precious truths about the character of God, and we will see His great faithfulness in keeping His promises. We will learn, in short, what it means to follow God wholeheartedly and walk by faith.

TITLE

First and Second Kings were considered one book in the earliest Hebrew manuscripts. They were later divided into two books by the translators of the Greek version, known as the Septuagint. This division was later followed by the Latin Vulgate, English translations, and modern Hebrew Bibles. The earliest Hebrew manuscripts titled the one book *Kings*, after the first word in verse 1. The books of 1 and 2 Samuel and 1 and 2 Kings combined represent a chronicle of the entire history of Judah's and Israel's kingship from Saul to Zedekiah.

AUTHOR AND DATE

Jewish tradition proposed that Jeremiah wrote Kings. However, this is unlikely because Jeremiah never went to Babylon where the final event of the book takes place, and the date this event took place (561 BC) would have made him at least eighty-six years old at the time. Based on the fact 1 and 2 Kings emphasize the ministry of prophets, it seems likely it was written by an unnamed prophet who lived during the exile. The evidence seems to point to a single author living in Babylon who drew from pre-exilic source materials to complete the books.

The last narrated event in 2 Kings 25:27–30 sets the earliest possible date of completion, and because there is no record of the end of the Babylonian captivity in Kings, the Israelites' release from exile identifies the latest possible writing date. This sets the date for the works between 561–538 BC. This date is sometimes challenged on the basis of the "to this day" statements throughout the books, but it is best to understand these as coming from sources the author used rather than by the author himself.

BACKGROUND AND SETTING

The action in 1 and 2 Kings takes place in the whole land of Israel, from Dan to Beersheba, including the Transjordan. The author tells of four invading nations who played a dominant role in the affairs of Israel and Judah from 971 to 561 BC. The first was Egypt, who impacted Israel's history during the tenth century BC. The second was Syria (Aram), who posed a threat during the ninth century BC. The third was Assyria, who terrorized Palestine from the mid-eighth century to the late seventh century BC and ultimately destroyed the northern kingdom of Israel in 722 BC. The fourth was Babylon, who became the dominant power from 612 to 539 BC. The Babylonians destroyed Jerusalem in 586 BC, carrying the people of Judah into captivity.

The author of Kings, an exile in Babylon, wrote the book to communicate the lessons of Israel's history—from the ascension of Solomon in 971 BC to the destruction of Jerusalem in 586 BC—to the Jews living in exile. To accomplish this, he traced the histories of two sets of kings and two nations of disobedient people—Israel and Judah—to show how the people grew indifferent to God's law and His prophets. The sad reality he reveals is that all the kings of Israel and the majority of the kings of Judah were apostates who led their people into idolatry. Because of the kings' failure, God sent His prophets to confront the people with their sin. When this message was rejected, the people were ultimately carried into exile.

HISTORICAL AND THEOLOGICAL THEMES

The book of 1 Kings covers the events of Solomon's reign, followed by the divided kingdoms of Israel and Judah, and the eventual decline and fall of both kingdoms. Each king is introduced with (1) his name and relation to his predecessor, (2) his date of accession, (3) his age in coming to the throne (for kings of Judah only), (4) his length of reign, (5) his place of reign, (6) his mother's name (for Judah only), and (7) the author's spiritual appraisal of his reign. This introduction is followed by a narration of the events that occurred during the reign of each king. Each reign is concluded with (1) a citation of sources, (2) additional historical notes, (3) notice of death, (4) notice of burial, (5) the name of the successor, and (6) in a few instances, an added postscript.

Three theological themes are emphasized in Kings. The first is that the Lord judged Israel and Judah because of their disobedience to His law. This unfaithfulness on the part of the rebellious people was furthered by the apostasy of the evil kings who led them into idolatry, which caused the Lord to exercise His righteous wrath against them.

A second theme is that the word of the true prophets always came to pass. Several times we are led to understand the narrated events happened "according to the word of the LORD which He had spoken by His servants the prophets" (2 Kings 24:2; see also 1 Kings 13:2–3; 22:15–28; 2 Kings 23:16). The Lord always kept His Word, even His warnings of judgment.

A third theme is that the Lord remembered His promise to David (see 1 Kings 11:12; 15:4; 2 Kings 8:19). Even though the kings of the Davidic line proved to be disobedient, God did not bring David's family to an end. Even as the book closes, the line of David still exists, so there is hope for the coming "seed" of David (see 2 Samuel 7:12–16).

INTERPRETIVE CHALLENGES

The major interpretive challenge in 1 and 2 Kings concerns the *chronology of the kings of Israel and Judah*. Although the author provides abundant chronological data in the books, this information is difficult to interpret for two reasons. First, there seems to be inconsistencies in the information given. For instance, 1 Kings 16:23 states that Omri, king of Israel, began to reign in the thirty-first year of Asa, king of Judah, and that he reigned twelve years. However, according to 1 Kings 16:29, Omri was succeeded by his son Ahab in the thirty-eighth year of Asa, giving Omri a reign of only seven years, not twelve.

Second, extrabiblical sources (Greek, Assyrian, and Babylonian) seem to provide contrasting dates to those given in 1 and 2 Kings. For instance, Ahab and Jehu, kings of Israel, are believed to be mentioned in Assyrian records. Based on these records, Ahab's death can be fixed at 853 BC, and Jehu's reign at 841 BC. With these dates, it is possible to determine the date of the division of Israel from Judah was c. 931 BC, the fall of Samaria was 722 BC, and the fall of Jerusalem was 586 BC. However, when the total years of royal reigns in 1 and 2 Kings are added, the number for Israel is 241 years (not 210) and for Judah is 393 years (not 346).

The solution to this problem is to recognize there were some co-regencies in both kingdoms—a period when two kings ruled at the same time—so the overlapping years were counted twice in the total for both kings. Further, different methods of reckoning the years of a king's rule and even different calendars were used at differing times in the two kingdoms, resulting in the seeming internal inconsistencies. The accuracy of the chronology in Kings can be demonstrated and confirmed.

A second major interpretive challenge deals with Solomon's relationship to the Abrahamic and Davidic covenants. Some interpret 1 Kings 4:20–21 as the fulfillment of the promises given to Abraham (see Genesis 15:18–21; 22:17). However, according to Numbers 34:6, the western border of the land promised to Abraham was the Mediterranean Sea. Furthermore, in 1 Kings 5:1, Hiram is an independent king of Tyre and deals with Solomon as an equal. Solomon's empire was not the fulfillment of the land promise given to Abraham by the Lord, though a great portion of that land was under Solomon's control.

Further, Solomon's statements in 1 Kings 5:5 and 8:20 seem to represent his claims to be the promised seed of the Davidic covenant, and the author of Kings holds out the possibility that Solomon's temple was the fulfillment of the Lord's promise to David. However, it is equally clear that Solomon did not meet the conditions required for the fulfillment of the promise to David (see 11:9–13). In fact, none of the historical kings in the house of David met the conditions of complete obedience that was to be the sign of the Promised One. The books of Kings thus point Israel to a future hope under the Messiah when the covenants would be fulfilled.

THE DIVIDED KINGDOM

Tyre
Dan
Damascus

Zarepath
PHOENICIA
Kedesh
ARAM
(SYRIA)
Hazor

Acco

Sea of
Galilee

Mt.
Carmel
River Kishon
Mt. Tabor
River Yarmuk

Megiddo
Jezreel
R. Jezreel

Taanach
Beth Shean
Ramoth Gilead

Jabesh Gilead

Great
Sea
Tirzah
Samaria
Mt. Ebal
Shechem
River Jordan
Penuel
River Jabbok
AMMON

Mt. Gerizim
Succoth

Aphek
Shiloh
ISRAEL

Joppa
Rabbah

Bethel
Jericho
Mt. Nebo
Heshbon

Gezer
Ashdod
Jerusalem
Medeba

Bethlehem

Gath
Adullam
Tekoa

Ashkelon
Dibon

Gaza
Hebron
Dead
Sea
River Arnon

PHILISTIA
Debir

JUDAH
MOAB

Arad

Beersheba
Kir Hareseth

△ = Mountains
Brook Zered
EDOM

Israel Splits in Two

1 Kings 12:1–24

Drawing Near

Why is it important today for companies to quickly address any complaints they receive from their customers? What happens if they don't practice good customer service?

_____

_____

_____

The Context

Near the end of David's reign, he appointed his son Solomon to succeed him as king, even though Solomon was not the next in line for kingship. Once the succession was secure, Solomon began his reign on a good footing. He asked God to grant him wisdom and received not only this gift but also great riches and power. Solomon would rule as Israel's king for forty years, and during his reign Israel would grow to become a powerful nation. At Solomon's death, all twelve tribes of Israel functioned together as one nation—but this situation would soon change.

Although Solomon had great wisdom and Israel prospered under him, he also had many ambitious plans for the nation. In order to make those plans come to pass, he resorted to using conscripted labor and levied heavy taxes on the people. When Solomon died and his son Rehoboam took the throne, the people hoped the change in kingship would give them some relief. So they approached their new king and requested that he ease their taxes and remove the burden of forced labor from their shoulders.

Rehoboam was forty-one years old when he took the throne, and the men who had advised his father were considerably older. But Rehoboam also brought along his own counselors—young men who had grown up with him and had been his personal friends. These men had probably been raised under privileged circumstances and had enjoyed the benefits of royal favor all their lives. Like Rehoboam, they had no firsthand experience in the affairs of governing Israel, and they lacked the wisdom of the elders who had advised Solomon.

The young king turned to his counselors for advice concerning the people's complaint, which demonstrated wisdom on his part. Unfortunately, he made the choice of following the counsel of his young friends, who turned out to be unwise advisors in this instance. In this way, Rehoboam proved to be an equally unwise king—and the nation suffered as a result.

KEYS TO THE TEXT

Read 1 Kings 12:1–24, noting the key words and phrases indicated below.

THE PEOPLE'S COMPLAINT: Rehoboam, Solomon's son, becomes king after his father's death. The people of Israel come to him with a request, and he is faced with a decision.

12:1. REHOBOAM WENT TO SHECHEM: Rehoboam was the son of Solomon and Naamah the Ammonite, who was the only wife of Solomon in the Hebrew Bible to be mentioned as having borne a child. Rehoboam's name meant "he who enlarges the people," though his reign would actually prove to divide the nation.

ALL ISRAEL HAD GONE TO SHECHEM: The representatives of the ten northern tribes had assembled in the city of Shechem to accept Rehoboam as king. Shechem was located in the hill country of northern Ephraim, approximately thirty miles north of Jerusalem, and had a long and important history as a political and religious center (see Joshua 24).

2. WHEN JEROBOAM THE SON OF BEBAT HEARD IT: Jeroboam was from Ephraim, the leading tribe of Israel's ten northern tribes. He was a man of talent who had served Solomon as leader over the building works around Jerusalem. When Solomon learned the prophet Ahijah had told Jeroboam that God would give him part of the kingdom, he sought to put Jeroboam to death. Jeroboam had fled to Egypt, and he was still there when word reached him that Solomon had died (see 1 Kings 11:26–43).

3. JEROBOAM AND THE WHOLE ASSEMBLY: The ten northern tribes summoned Jeroboam from Egypt to become their representative and spokesman in their dealings with Rehoboam.

4. YOUR FATHER MADE OUR YOKE HEAVY: Apparently, Solomon's harsh policies were the central issue on the minds of the people—much as the economy and taxes figure prominently in people's politics today—and they were willing to follow Solomon's son if he simply lessened those burdens. However, the Lord's concerns were not with Israel's financial economy but with the spiritual condition of her leaders.

6. THE ELDERS: Solomon's counselors and cabinet ministers. These men would probably have been a good deal older than Rehoboam, since they had served when his father was king.

7. IF YOU WILL BE A SERVANT TO THESE PEOPLE: The elders gave Rehoboam good counsel. A wise king must be a servant to his people—a principle that the Lord of Creation Himself demonstrated when He washed His disciples' feet. The people's request was not excessive, and Rehoboam could have granted it without much sacrifice.

8. THE YOUNG MEN WHO HAD GROWN UP WITH HIM: Rehoboam had evidently surrounded himself with his friends, and perhaps even created offices for them to fill. It was wise of Rehoboam to seek counsel before making a decision, but it would have been far wiser if he had listened to the advice of those who were older and more experienced in the court of Solomon.

10. THICKER THAN MY FATHER'S WAIST: Rehoboam's young counselors quoted this proverb of the time, implying that Rehoboam's most lenient measures should be more severe and powerful than Solomon's strongest measures. In this way, they foolishly counseled the king to exert his power over the people and not listen to their demands.

11. MY FATHER CHASTISED YOU WITH WHIPS, BUT I WILL CHASTISE YOU WITH SCOURGES: A whip is a single cord of leather, but a scourge had many cords attached—often with bits of bone or sharp stone at the ends to tear the flesh. The implication was that Rehoboam's burden on the people would be far more severe and cutting than what they had experienced under Solomon.

14. HE SPOKE TO THEM ACCORDING TO THE ADVICE OF THE YOUNG MEN: Rehoboam's attitude toward his power was despotic and not in keeping with the specific model the Lord had given concerning His chosen king. God had commanded, "[A king] shall not multiply horses for himself, nor cause the people to return to Egypt to multiply horses. . . . Neither shall he multiply wives for himself, lest his heart turn away. . . . He shall read [the law] all the days of his life, that he may learn to fear the LORD his God and be careful to observe all the words of this law and these statutes, that his heart may not be lifted above his brethren, that he may not turn aside from the commandment to the right hand or to the left" (Deuteronomy 17:16–17, 19–20).

THE PEOPLE REBEL: Rehoboam's response turns the people of Israel against him, and the kingdom divides into two separate nations.

15. THE TURN OF EVENTS WAS FROM THE LORD: From a human perspective, Rehoboam might have prevented the national division simply by listening to the people and to the wise advice of his elders. However, from this verse we see that God had already determined the division should take place so "that He might fulfill His word." God sovereignly used the foolishness of Rehoboam to fulfill Ahijah's prophecy (see 1 Kings 11:29–39).

16. WHAT SHARE HAVE WE IN DAVID: A man named Sheba had once rebelled against King David using almost identical words as his rallying cry: "We have no share in David" (2 Samuel 20:1). The people of the ten northern tribes of Israel were thus openly rejecting David and his descendants as their rightful king. However, the people of Judah would remain loyal to the house of David and accept Rehoboam as their king.

17. THE CHILDREN OF ISRAEL: These were people from the northern tribes who had migrated south and settled in Judah.

18. ADORAM, WHO WAS IN CHARGE OF THE REVENUE: Adoram, also called Adoniram, had been the overseer for forced labor and taxation throughout

Israel under both David and Solomon (see 2 Samuel 20:24; 1 Kings 4:6). From a human standpoint, it was probably a foolish tactic for Rehoboam to send the overseer of forced labor to negotiate with the men of Israel. However, we must remember the Lord was in control of all these events, and He was guiding this situation intentionally to lead to the split in the kingdom.

ALL ISRAEL STONED HIM WITH STONES: Killing such a high court official was an act of open revolution against the king. The men who committed this act presumably would not hesitate to murder Rehoboam himself as well. Even though God had planned to divide the kingdom, the men of Israel were not justified in committing this crime.

19. ISRAEL HAS BEEN IN REBELLION: God's Word teaches us that rebellion is the same as the sin of witchcraft (see 1 Samuel 15:23). We must recognize the Lord was bringing about the fulfillment of His determination to split the nation, but He still was not pleased by the sinful actions of His people. God may choose to use the wicked deeds of men to accomplish His purposes, but that does not exonerate those who commit the deeds.

20. MADE HIM KING OVER ALL ISRAEL: It is interesting that the people of Israel (the ten northern tribes) evidently anointed Jeroboam as king without involving the priests. Up to this point, the Lord had anointed each king of Israel through His priests, which indicated that He Himself had chosen the king. However, in this case there is no indication that the people even consulted the Lord on the matter.

REHOBOAM'S REPRISAL: Rehoboam flees back to Jerusalem, where he raises an army to reassert control over the northern tribes. But God has a word for him.

21. HE ASSEMBLED ALL THE HOUSE OF JUDAH: Simeon, the tribe originally given land in the southern section of Judah's territory (see Joshua 19:1–9), had apparently migrated north by this time and was counted with the ten northern tribes. Thus, the ten northern tribes were Reuben, Simeon, Zebulun, Issachar, Dan, Gad, Asher, Naphtali, Manasseh, and Ephraim. The only tribe to remain completely loyal to the house of David was Judah, while Benjamin, the twelfth tribe, was split between the two kingdoms. The tribe of Levi, originally scattered throughout both kingdoms, resided in Judah during the divided kingdom era.

22. THE MAN OF GOD: This is a common Old Testament expression to designate a man with a message from God who would speak authoritatively on the Lord's behalf. Moses himself had been called "the man of God" (Deuteronomy 33:1).

24. THIS THING IS FROM ME: Through the prophet Shemaiah, the Lord commanded Rehoboam and his army not to invade Israel. God, in judgment, had ordained the north-south split, so to attack Israel was to oppose God Himself. Once again, however, we must remember that God had not ordained the method of the rebellion and the murderous deeds committed by some of the people.

THEY OBEYED THE WORD OF THE LORD: To their credit, Rehoboam and the people of Judah heeded the words of Shemaiah and did not go to war against the northern tribes. In 2 Chronicles 11:5–12, we read that Rehoboam went back to Jerusalem and fortified many of the cities in the southern kingdom in case of attack from the north. "In every city he put shields and spears, and made them very strong, having Judah and Benjamin on his side" (verse 12).

UNLEASHING THE TEXT

1) If you had been in Rehoboam's position, how might you have responded to the Israelites' complaints? Why was it tempting for Rehoboam to follow the advice of his friends?

_____

_____

_____

2) In what sense would Rehoboam have been a servant to the people if he had granted their requests? What role was he taking on when he refused to meet their needs?

_____

_____

_____

3) In your opinion, what reasons might Rehoboam have had in setting up friends of his own age as his counselors? Why did he also retain the elders?

_____

_____

_____

4) Why did the people of Israel murder Adoram? Why did they reject Rehoboam? What should their response have been?

_____

_____

_____

EXPLORING THE MEANING

The Lord calls us to serve one another. Rehoboam's elder counselors advised him to "be a servant to these people today, and serve them, and answer them, and speak good words to them" (1 Kings 12:7). Their counsel was wise, and Rehoboam should have heeded it. While the Scriptures show that humility makes a person receptive to grace, the world would have us believe that humility is a sign of inferiority or weakness. This evidently was Rehoboam's mistaken mindset, for he strove to demonstrate his power and majesty by threatening to be even harsher and more demanding than his father.

Jesus provides us with the opposite example. He is the King of kings and Lord of lords. He was more powerful and majestic than the greatest kings who ever lived, yet He bowed Himself before His own servants and humbly washed their feet (see John 13:1–17). The Lord also commanded His disciples to follow His example. They were to be willing to serve one another even in such lowly occupations as washing one another's feet.

Servanthood is not an option or something that some are "called to do" while others are not—it is a command the Lord gives to all His followers. If we want to follow Him, we must obey Him, and part of that obedience includes being a willing servant to others. "If I then, your Lord and Teacher, have washed your feet, you also ought to wash one another's feet. For I have given you an example, that you should do as I have done to you" (John 13:14–15).

Rebellion is like the sin of witchcraft. The people of Israel rebelled against Rehoboam, even though God had chosen him to be Solomon's successor to the throne. It is true the Lord used this act of rebellion to accomplish His own purposes, but we must not lose sight of the fact that the people's rebellion was sinful in God's eyes.

The Lord, through the prophet Samuel, had declared that "rebellion is as the sin of witchcraft, and stubbornness is as iniquity and idolatry" (1 Samuel 15:23). Lucifer committed rebellion against God when he raised himself up to be equal with God (see Isaiah 14:12–15), and those who rebel against God's chosen authority effectively follow in the devil's footsteps. When we rebel against the Lord, we are removing Him from authority in our lives and setting ourselves in His place. This is essentially what the people of Israel did when they threw down Rehoboam and set up a man of their own choosing.

Christians are called to submit themselves both to the Lord and to those whom He has placed in authority over them. Jesus, the Lord of the universe, voluntarily submitted Himself to the religious and political authorities of His day—even to the point of allowing them to crucify Him. As Peter wrote, "Submit yourselves to every ordinance of man for the Lord's sake, whether to the king as supreme, or to governors, as to those who are sent by him for the punishment of evildoers and for the praise of those who do good" (1 Peter 2:13–14).

Divine sovereignty does not nullify human responsibility. The Lord prophesied that He would tear the kingdom away from Solomon's son and divide the nation of Israel into two separate kingdoms. He used the foolish decisions of Rehoboam and the rebellious spirit of Israel to accomplish this purpose—yet this did not exonerate Rehoboam from culpability for his foolishness or the people of Israel for their sin. God is indeed sovereign over all the affairs of humankind, but this does not mean He will not judge individuals for their actions.

Jesus again provides the perfect example of this principle. It was God's plan from the foundation of the world that His perfect Son should offer Himself as a sacrifice to redeem sinful men, and God used the evil deeds of those who rejected Christ to accomplish that plan. Yet this did not exonerate those who crucified Christ for their deeds. In the same way, it does not exonerate anyone who rejects Jesus as the only way to salvation and peace with God.

The good news is that God uses all things to further His purposes in our lives. When we live in obedience to His Word, we can rest in the assurance that God is completely sovereign over all the events and circumstances that come our way, and He will turn all things to His glory and our blessing. "All things work together for good to those who love God, to those who are the called according to His purpose" (Romans 8:28).

REFLECTING ON THE TEXT

5) Why did God permit the people to commit rebellion and murder? Why does His sovereign use of such deeds not exonerate people from personal responsibility?

---

6) What reasons might Rehoboam have had for answering the people in such harsh terms? What might he have hoped to accomplish? What was wrong with his thinking?

---

7) Why did God choose to split the kingdom into two parts? At what points might He have chosen to not do so? What human actions moved Him in that direction?

_____

_____

_____

_____

8) Why did God say that rebellion is like the sin of witchcraft? How are the two sins related? What does this suggest about the seriousness of a rebellious spirit?

_____

_____

_____

PERSONAL RESPONSE

9) Do you generally prefer to serve or to be served? Which role tends to characterize your life more? To what areas of service might the Lord be calling you?

_____

_____

_____

_____

10) How do you generally respond to authority? Are there areas of rebellion in your life? What needs to change in your thinking or your actions?

_____

_____

_____

THE KINGS OF ISRAEL AND JUDAH (C. 930–848 BC)

King of Israel	Reign (BC)*	Length (years)
Jeroboam I	930–910	22
Nadab	910–909	2
Baasha	909–886	24
Elah	886–885	2
Zimri	885	(7 days)
Omri	885–874	12
Ahab	874–853	22
Pekah	740 (752)–732	20
Hoshea	732–722	9
10 northern tribes enter captivity	722	
King of Judah	Reign (BC)*	Length (years)
Rehoboam	931–913	17
Abijam (Abijah)	913–911	3
Asa	911–870	41
Jehoshaphat	870 (873)–848	25

*All dates are approximate. Dates in parentheses indicate a co-regency of father and son.

2

THE FEARS OF JEROBOAM

1 Kings 12:25–13:34

DRAWING NEAR

In what ways can fear lead people to doubt that the Lord will take of them? How can fear cause otherwise rational people to act in an irrational manner?

_____

_____

_____

_____

THE CONTEXT

As we saw in our last study, the people of Israel rejected Rehoboam, Solomon's son, as their king when he treated them disgracefully. In his place, they elevated Jeroboam to the throne and swore their allegiance to him. These events, of course, did not catch the Lord by surprise, for it was all part of His plan for the nation of Israel.

The Lord had even promised Jeroboam that his authority would be secure and his sons would follow him on the throne. He had told Jeroboam through the prophet Ahijah, "I will take the kingdom out of [Solomon's] hand and give it to you—ten tribes. And to his son I will give one tribe, that My servant David may always have a lamp before Me in Jerusalem, the city which I have chosen for Myself, to put My name there. So I will take you, and you shall reign over all your heart desires, and you shall be king over Israel" (1 Kings 11:35–37).

So Jeroboam had nothing to fear as he took command. All that God required Jeroboam to do was obey His Word and follow His commands, and He would assure the new king of blessing and success. But Jeroboam refused to believe this was the truth. Instead, he convinced himself the people of Israel would turn against him once they got a chance, change their minds, and return to Rehoboam—and kill him in the process. These fears were groundless, for there was no indication, as far as we are told in the Bible, that the people even entertained such thoughts. Essentially, Jeroboam was doubting the Word of God.

Fear is often like this. It ignores facts and logic and takes control of our hearts and minds—if we allow it to do so. Jeroboam allowed his fears to guide him, and as a result he walked into grievous sin instead of walking into God's promises. What's worse, he led the entire nation of Israel into idolatry—and all because he did not trust in the Lord's faithfulness.

KEYS TO THE TEXT

Read 1 Kings 12:25–13:34, noting the key words and phrases indicated below.

KING JEROBOAM BECOMES AFRAID: Jeroboam persuades himself that the Israelites will turn against him if they travel to Jerusalem to offer sacrifices in the temple. So he concocts a wicked scheme.

12:25. JEROBOAM BUILT SHECHEM . . . AND BUILT PENUEL: Jeroboam fortified the city of Shechem, located in the hill country north of Jerusalem, and made it into his royal residence. He also fortified Penuel, situated on the River Jabbok directly to the west. Jeroboam apparently intended to establish his authority over the people of Israel on both sides of the Jordan River.

26. JEROBOAM SAID IN HIS HEART: As we have seen, God had offered Jeroboam complete security for his throne and for his posterity if he obeyed the Lord's commands and followed in His ways (see 1 Kings 11:38). But Jeroboam's heart was not turned toward God, and he did not place his trust in the Lord's faithfulness. He allowed his fears—that the people would return to Rehoboam as king—to lead him into sin.

27. THE HOUSE OF THE LORD AT JERUSALEM: The Lord had ordained a political, not a religious, division of Solomon's kingdom. Jeroboam was to religiously follow the Mosaic Law, which demanded that he follow the Lord's direction for the *entire* nation of Israel to worship and offer sacrifices at the temple in Jerusalem. God had previously instructed Solomon to build this temple, and the ark of the covenant, which represented the Lord's presence with His people, was housed there. Jeroboam's lack of trust in God's faithfulness actually led him to assume that if the people walked in obedience to the Lord's commands, they would remove him from the throne—even though the Lord had placed him there in the first place. This cockeyed reasoning motivated him set up a place of worship in the north.

A MORE COMFORTABLE RELIGION: Jeroboam seduces the people of Israel to join him in idolatry by offering them an easier and less costly way of worship.

28. TWO CALVES OF GOLD: Jeroboam presented two calves, which were probably made of wood overlaid with gold, to Israel as pedestals on which the Lord supposedly sat or stood. Aaron had previously set up a golden calf during Israel's exodus from Egypt, and the Lord's wrath had burned fiercely when the people bowed in worship before it (see Exodus 32). Jeroboam presented his golden calves to the people using almost the exact same words that Aaron had used: "This is your god, O Israel, that brought you out of the land of Egypt!" (Exodus 32:4).

IT IS TOO MUCH FOR YOU: Jeroboam presented three arguments in support of his idolatrous plan: (1) worshiping the Lord in Jerusalem was inconvenient, and the calves would make worship less burdensome; (2) the calves were actually gods, containing some mystical power to protect and forgive the people; and (3) the people's ancestors did it, so it must be right. These three lies are still prevalent in the world today, and even Christians can fall prey to them. The church, too, often disregards Scripture's teachings in favor of that which seems expedient, less inconvenient, or more "relevant." The world claims that every religious system has something to offer, and we are pressured to place our faith in just about anything but the Word of God. But false religions have been around for a long time, as have the lies of the Evil One, and the antiquity of a belief system does not mean that it is true.

29. HE SET UP ONE IN BETHEL, AND THE OTHER HE PUT IN DAN: Bethel was located near the southern border of his kingdom, about eleven miles north of Jerusalem. The people had long revered the area as a sacred place because Jacob had worshiped there (see Genesis 28:10–22; 35:1–15). Dan was located in the northernmost part of Jeroboam's kingdom, about twenty-five miles north of the Sea of Galilee. The people had practiced a paganized worship of the Lord in this region during the period of the judges (see Judges 18:30–31). Jeroboam had thus gone out of his way to make his false religion as convenient as possible, and the country was now bracketed by cow worship rather than God worship.

30. THIS THING BECAME A SIN: It is unquestionably a sin to set up golden calves and tell people they are gods, but Jeroboam's position as king gave his lies greater authority. His actions ultimately led the entire nation of Israel to fall into sin and idolatry.

31. SHRINES ON THE HIGH PLACES: The "high places" were hilltop sanctuaries the Canaanites had used for their pagan worship practices. When the Israelites entered the Promised Land, the Lord had commanded them to "drive out all the inhabitants of the land . . . destroy all their engraved stones, destroy all their molded images, and demolish all their high places" (Numbers 33:52). God's people were to worship Him only at the temple once Solomon had constructed it. Yet Solomon himself had ignored this command, and now we see the fruit of that choice being borne under his successors. These high places would continue to plague the nation of Israel throughout the reign of its kings.

INVENTING A NEW RELIGION: *The king appoints his own priesthood for his new religion and even invents a special holiday— to coincide with God's chosen feast.*

PRIESTS FROM EVERY CLASS OF PEOPLE: Here we discover another crafty technique Jeroboam used in selling his false religion: he removed "class boundaries" and made the priesthood available to everyone. The Lord, however, had expressly chosen only the men who were descended from Aaron as

His priests, who were members of the tribe of Levi (see Numbers 3:10). This move on Jeroboam's part was another act of expediency, as under his false religion he could call on people who lived near his many shrines, rather than strictly Levites, to act as priests.

32. JEROBOAM ORDAINED A FEAST: Jeroboam ordered this feast to be held "on the fifteenth day of the eighth month," at around the same time as the Feast of the Tabernacles in Jerusalem. In this way, Jeroboam was deliberately trying to compete with God's ordained time of worship. He was raising himself far above his proper kingly authority—to the point that he was ordaining religious festivals as though he were in the place of God.

HE INSTALLED THE PRIESTS OF THE HIGH PLACES: According to 2 Chronicles 11:13–15, Jeroboam rejected all the priests and Levites from the ten northern tribes because he feared their loyalty to Jerusalem and the temple. In their place he appointed his own idolatrous priests, with the result that all the true priests moved south and found refuge in Judah with Rehoboam. The author of Chronicles states that Jeroboam appointed these priests "for the demons," which was another term for idols (see Leviticus 17:7).

33. HE MADE OFFERINGS ON THE ALTAR: Jeroboam also took upon himself the role of a priest, just as Saul had done several generations earlier (see 1 Samuel 13). The Lord had rejected Saul for his sinful presumption, yet Jeroboam's act was even more depraved, because he was acting as a priest before the idols he had created.

CONFRONTED BY A PROPHET: *The Lord sends a man of God to confront the king, who prophesies that God's judgment will fall on Jeroboam for his apostasy.*

13:1. A MAN OF GOD WENT FROM JUDAH: The Lord sent a prophet from the nation loyal to David's line to rebuke the now idolatrous north. This would add extra insult to the rebuke the prophet was about to bring.

2. JOSIAH BY NAME: Josiah would become king in Judah some 300 years after this prophecy. The prophet predicted that he would slaughter the illegitimate priests of the high places of his day who made offerings on the altar at Bethel. This prophecy was ultimately realized when King Josiah executed the divine judgment on the non-Levitical priesthood established by Jeroboam (see 2 Kings 22–23).

3. HE GAVE A SIGN: In Deuteronomy 18:22, God told His people, "When a prophet speaks in the name of the LORD, if the thing does not happen or come to pass, that is the thing which the LORD has not spoken." As a sign that this prophet's long-term prediction would come to pass—and that he was thus speaking the word of the Lord—God provided the immediate "wonder" of the altar splitting apart (see 2 Kings 13:5).

4. THEN HIS HAND . . . WITHERED: When Jeroboam heard the prophecy he tried to arrest the man of God. However, the Lord miraculously intervened by removing the vitality from the very hand that was reaching out against God's prophet. This dramatic sign also demonstrated that Jeroboam's kingly power would soon wither up as well.

5. THE ALTAR ALSO WAS SPLIT APART: The torn altar was a clear and visible demonstration of the way God destroys all false idols. The ashes spilling on the ground indicated that even the offerings and sacrifices that had been made on that altar were contemptible and deserved to be trampled underfoot by men and animals alike.

6. PRAY FOR ME: The roles were reversed between the mighty king and the lowly prophet when Jeroboam stretched out his hand and asked for healing. The king would have been unlikely to show any mercy to the prophet, but in contrast the Lord demonstrated His great mercy by restoring the king's hand to its former health. Strangely enough, in spite of the miraculous events Jeroboam had seen, he refused to repent.

8. I WOULD NOT GO IN WITH YOU: Jeroboam made a great show of offering reward and fellowship to the man of God—perhaps to show the people of Israel that he once again had God's blessing. However, in that day the act of sharing a meal with another man indicated intimate fellowship. The prophet thus refused to dine with the king, because the Lord would have no communion with Jeroboam's false gods.

No Exceptions: The Lord requires obedience from all His people, regardless of whether they are kings or prophets. The man of God learns this lesson too late.

9. COMMANDED ME BY THE WORD OF THE LORD: The man of God's divine commission expressly forbade him from receiving any

hospitality at Bethel. The commission even required him to return home by a different route from the one by which he came, lest he should be recognized. The prophet's own conduct was to symbolize the Lord's total rejection of Israel's false worship and the recognition that all the people had become apostates.

11. AN OLD PROPHET DWELT IN BETHEL: This spokesman for the Lord had compromised his ministry through his willingness to live at the very center of the false system of worship without speaking out against it.

18. HE WAS LYING TO HIM: The text does not state why the old prophet chose to deceive the man of God. It may be that his own sons were worshipers at Bethel or perhaps priests, and he wanted to gain favor with the king by showing up the man of God as an imposter who acted contrary to his own claim to have heard from God. The Judean prophet, who was accustomed to receiving direct revelations from the Lord, should have regarded this supposed angelic message with suspicion and sought divine verification of this revised order.

20. THE WORD OF THE LORD: The old prophet's lie arose from his own imagination, but the true prophecy came from the Lord.

22. YOUR CORPSE SHALL NOT COME TO THE TOMB OF YOUR FATHERS: The Israelites buried their dead with the bones of their ancestors in a common grave (see Judges 8:32). The lack of such a burial was considered a severe punishment and disgrace.

24. STOOD BY THE CORPSE: The Lord's prophecy against the man of God quickly came to pass when a lion met him on the road and killed him. Both the man's donkey and the lion acted unnaturally after the attack, for the donkey did not run away and the lion did not attack the donkey or disturb the man's body. Unlike the disobedient prophet, the beasts bent their will to God's sovereignty.

32. WILL SURELY COME TO PASS: The old prophet of Bethel instructed his sons to bury him beside the Judean prophet. In making this statement, he reveals that he was finally willing to identify himself with the message the man of God had given against worship at Bethel.

33. AGAIN HE MADE PRIESTS: Unlike the old prophet, Jeroboam did not change his evil ways but continued to appoint priests outside the tribe of Levi to serve in the high places.

UNLEASHING THE TEXT

1) Why did Jeroboam create the golden calves? What motivated him to do such a thing?

_____

_____

_____

_____

2) What tactics did Jeroboam use to seduce the people of Israel into worshiping his calves? How does the world apply similar pressures to God's people today?

_____

_____

_____

_____

3) Why did the man of God refuse the king's gifts? Why did he decline to eat with the king? What does this show about God's attitude toward idolatry?

_____

_____

_____

_____

4) What caused the man of God to disobey the Lord's instructions not to accept any hospitality in Bethel? How did this mistake lead to his death?

_____

_____

_____

_____

EXPLORING THE MEANING

Fear often comes from doubts about God. Jeroboam's fear led him to believe the people of Israel would turn against him once they began traveling to Jerusalem to worship. His fears for his throne, his kingdom, and his very life led him to take rash steps in self-defense—even though nobody had actually threatened him. He set up false idols and invented a whole new religion simply because he feared the Israelites would turn against him if they worshiped God in Jerusalem as the Lord had commanded them to do.

The reality was that God had solemnly promised Jeroboam that his throne would be secure, both for himself and for his descendants, if he walked in compliance with His stated will. Jeroboam had nothing to fear whatsoever. Even if some people had decided in the future to turn against his authority, the Lord would have preserved him just as He did David.

Fear causes us to move away from the Lord, not toward Him. Anxiety and worry are symptoms of a lack of trust in God's faithfulness, because God always keeps His promises. The antidote to fear is to meditate on God's promises and remind ourselves that the Bible promises He will always be faithful. Jeroboam would have avoided grievous sin if he had believed in God's promises—and he would not have led the entire nation of Israel into apostasy.

Christians must honor the Lord's commands concerning spiritual headship. There is a certain irony in Jeroboam's decision to create a new priesthood in Israel. He was afraid the people would rebel against his authority, even though

God had ordained him, and he dealt with that imagined threat by rebelling against God's chosen priestly authority.

The Lord had commanded that only men from the tribe of Levi could become priests, but that didn't fit with Jeroboam's plan to keep the people of Israel away from Jerusalem. So he ignored that stipulation and appointed his own priesthood from every class of people within Israel—people he undoubtedly selected for their willingness to disregard God's commands. In the minds of such people, the Lord's stipulations for spiritual authority had ceased to be relevant, so it was perfectly acceptable for them to rewrite those laws.

The church today faces the same pressures in this regard. God's Word is clear on the subject of having qualified leadership within the local church and male headship within the home, but the world pressures Christians to disregard those directions as being outdated and no longer relevant. God's people must not be led away from His Word. The Lord wants men to rise up and take the lead in their churches and in their homes, regardless of what the world around them thinks.

Stand guard against idolatry. As we have seen, King Jeroboam's fears that the Israelites would abandon him if they traveled to Jerusalem to worship the Lord led him to create idols for the people to worship instead. In fact, he went well beyond this by creating an entire religious system around his golden calves. He appointed priests, established several centers of worship, and even created a special feast day for his newly invented religion.

Jeroboam clearly committed idolatry when he constructed two golden calves and set them up for public adoration. Yet his idolatry was even craftier and subtler than that, and his actions illustrate the ways in which the world pressures Christians to create their own golden calves. Our own interests can become idols in our lives that motivate us to depart from obedience to God's Word, even as Jeroboam did out of concern for his own kingship.

Career goals, financial aspirations, dreams of the future, worldly prestige, and many other concerns can creep into our hearts like an insidious vine and choke out our commitment to the Lord. It is even possible to allow something that is legitimate and good in its own right to become so important in our hearts that it becomes an idol. Anything that takes priority over God's Word can become a golden calf in our lives. As the Lord said, "You shall have no other gods before Me. . . . For I, the LORD your God, am a jealous God" (Exodus 20:3, 5).

REFLECTING ON THE TEXT

5) Why did Jeroboam fall into fear? How did the fear influence his judgment? How might he have avoided this whole situation?

_____

_____

_____

_____

6) In what ways did Solomon's failure to destroy the high places have an influence in Jeroboam's day? How might things have been different if Solomon had obeyed God in this matter?

_____

_____

_____

7) What idols do people worship in the modern world?

_____

_____

_____

_____

8) What does Scripture teach about a man's responsibilities in the home? About his responsibilities in the church? How do these teachings compare with the world's beliefs?

_____

_____

_____

_____

PERSONAL RESPONSE

9) Are there any idols in your life? What things threaten to compete with your devotion to the Lord? How can you remove those threats?

_____

_____

_____

_____

10) Do you tend to be fearful or anxious? What causes you to worry? What promises of God can you apply to those fears?

_____

_____

_____

_____

3

THE SIN OF SYNCRETISM
1 Kings 14:1–20

DRAWING NEAR

What are some ways that Christians today "mix" the teachings of the world with the teachings of God? What is the danger in not setting clear boundaries in certain areas of life?

_____

_____

_____

THE CONTEXT

Syncretism is the practice of combining the teachings of the world with the teachings of the Bible. For example, the world teaches the human race evolved from lower life forms over the course of many millions of years, while the Bible teaches God created the entire universe from nothing in six days. If we attempt to reconcile these two opposing viewpoints by altering the Word of God to accommodate the teachings of the world, we commit the sin of syncretism.

Jeroboam committed this sin when he created his own new religious system. As we saw in the previous study, he crafted two golden calves, encouraged the Israelites to pray to them, and then instituted his own order of priests to make sacrifices to the Lord *and* to the idols. Notice that in setting up this system he did not *abolish* worship of the one true God in Israel, but merely redesigned it to fit his own needs. In this way, he committed the sin of syncretism.

Syncretism is motivated by people's desires to live life their own way and worship God on their own terms. It may not involve a wholesale rejection of God's Word—just parts of it that don't fit their agendas. It might involve ignoring some principles, and it might include inventing new principles, but it ultimately involves rewriting God's Word in order to serve oneself—and that is a form of idolatry.

As we will see in this study, the Lord takes the sin of syncretism seriously. Jeroboam might have thought it was acceptable to mix Canaanite worship with the worship of the one God, but the Lord viewed all such acts as idolatry—and He would hold Jeroboam accountable for leading the people into sin. This judgment would come through Ahijah—the same prophet who had told Jeroboam that God had given him the throne of Israel.

KEYS TO THE TEXT

Read 1 Kings 14:1–20, noting the key words and phrases indicated below.

> JEROBOAM'S SON: *Shortly after Jeroboam institutes his own religious system in Israel, his son becomes gravely ill. In this moment of crisis, the king turns to God rather than his idols.*

1. AT THAT TIME: This indicates the events in this chapter took place shortly after the events recorded in 1 Kings 13, where Jeroboam "made priests from every class of people for the high places" (verse 33).

ABIJAH THE SON OF JEROBOAM: Abijah's name means "my father is the LORD." This suggests that his father, Jeroboam, wanted to be regarded as a worshiper of the Lord at the time of his birth—though God viewed the king's syncretistic practices as pure idolatry. Abijah was referred to as a "child" in this passage (see verses 3, 12, 17), a term that can be used of an individual from childhood through young adulthood. Of all of Jeroboam's family, Abijah was the most responsive to the Lord (see verse 13).

2. DISGUISE YOURSELF: Jeroboam evidently wanted to deceive both the prophet of God and the people of Israel. This suggests he was unwilling for the people to see him consulting a prophet of God rather than one of the priests he had appointed. After all, he had invented a new religious system for the people of Israel, telling them that they could incorporate idolatry into their worship practices and still please God. Yet the fact he consulted with Ahijah indicates he knew his own syncretistic religion to be worthless; in a time of crisis, he turned back to obedience to the Lord.

GO TO SHILOH: Shiloh was a town in Ephraim located about twenty miles north of Jerusalem. It was the location of the tabernacle that housed the ark of the covenant before Solomon built the temple in Jerusalem.

AHIJAH THE PROPHET: As we saw in a previous study, Ahijah had predicted the Lord would give Jeroboam the ten northern tribes (see 1 Kings 11:29–39). Ahijah had also told Jeroboam the Lord would establish his throne if he obeyed God's commands. Ahijah's prophecies had come to pass, which demonstrated he was a true man of God and not a false prophet.

3. TEN LOAVES: This simple food gift added to Jeroboam's disguise, as it would have been suitable for a common laborer, but not for a king. Jeroboam was hoping to deceive the prophet about his wife's identity, which demonstrates how deeply confused his thinking was. On one hand, he recognized that Ahijah was a prophet of God who was capable of predicting future events as revealed by the Lord. On the other hand, the king thought he could hide his wife's identity from such a man by the ruse of a simple disguise.

THE BLIND SEER: Ahijah is blind, but he doesn't need physical eyes to see the truth. The Lord gives him true spiritual sight, which cannot be deceived by silly disguises.

4. AHIJAH COULD NOT SEE: The irony here is that the disguise was completely wasted, because Ahijah couldn't see anyway. However, as we will see, the loss of his physical sight had no bearing on his spiritual sight.

5. HERE IS THE WIFE OF JEROBOAM: It is conceivable that the woman's disguise might have deceived Ahijah in his blindness, just as Jacob's disguise deceived Isaac (see Genesis 27), but God's eyes are never blinded. The Lord sees all things—in fact, He sees them more clearly and accurately than

any human eyes ever could. God was watching as Jeroboam's wife traveled on her deceitful errand, and His eyes were also on Jeroboam's sick son.

6. COME IN, WIFE OF JEROBOAM: Imagine how startled Jeroboam's wife must have been when she heard these words! Yet the greeting also served to let her know that the message Ahijah was about to deliver to her was from the Lord.

WHY DO YOU PRETEND TO BE ANOTHER PERSON: Jeroboam had been doing this very same thing—pretending to serve the God of Israel when in fact he was pursuing false gods. People may deceive themselves into thinking they are following the Word of God while actually pursuing their own ways, but God is not mocked. "Do not be deceived, God is not mocked; for whatever a man sows, that he will also reap" (Galatians 6:7).

GOD'S COMING JUDGMENT: The Lord prophesies through Ahijah that Jeroboam's son will die. Even worse, his entire house will be put to death because of his syncretism.

7. I EXALTED YOU: Jeroboam had not been born into a royal household, and he had no right (in earthly terms) to become king. But the Lord had lifted him up and given him responsibility for the ten northern tribes of Israel. The king's role was to lead God's people through example into obedience to the Lord's commands. However, Jeroboam had done just the opposite, leading Israel away from God by incorporating idolatry into Israel's proper worship practices.

8. TORE THE KINGDOM AWAY FROM THE HOUSE OF DAVID: David had been a man after God's own heart, and the Lord had established his throne forever. Yet He was willing to tear away the kingdom from David's descendants when Solomon did not remain faithful to the whole Word of God. How much more so, then, would the Lord be willing to tear it away from Jeroboam, who had not walked at all in His ways!

9. ALL WHO WERE BEFORE YOU: Jeroboam had failed to live up to the standard of David, and his wickedness had even surpassed that of Saul and Solomon. Solomon had followed the Lord with a divided heart, but Jeroboam's sin was even more immoral because he had installed a paganized system of worship for the entire population of the northern kingdom. In this way, he willfully led the nation away from the Lord's commands in order to strengthen his own position of power.

CAST ME BEHIND YOUR BACK: This is a powerful picture of the sin of syncretism. People effectively thrust God behind their back when they determine to add to and delete from the Word of God, thus making themselves the leader and God the follower—or, at least, when they attempt to do so. This is essentially the same sin that Lucifer committed when he sought to make himself equal with God (see Isaiah 14:12–14).

10. AS ONE TAKES AWAY REFUSE: The Lord was going to remove Jeroboam and his household from Israel as though He were throwing out the garbage. This is a powerful statement on how God views man's syncretistic practices. The Lord commands obedience to His Word as it is written, and any deviation from that is like smelly rubbish to Him.

11. DOGS SHALL EAT WHOEVER BELONGS TO JEROBOAM: At this time in Israel's history, it was a sign of being cursed by God if a person died and lay unburied. The Lord's wrath against Jeroboam was severe, yet He had warned His people this very fate would befall them if they adulterated their worship with pagan practices. "Your carcasses shall be food for all the birds of the air and the beasts of the earth, and no one shall frighten them away" (Deuteronomy 28:26).

13. WHO SHALL COME TO THE GRAVE: In other words, this was the only son of Jeroboam who would receive the honor of a proper burial.

IN HIM THERE IS FOUND SOMETHING GOOD TOWARD THE LORD: We are not told what the Lord saw in Abijah's character, but He did find something in the young man that pleased Him. The Lord's eyes are always on His children—not in hopes of searching out evil and sin, but in order to show Himself faithful and to bring blessing (see 2 Chronicles 16:9).

14. RAISE UP FOR HIMSELF A KING OVER ISRAEL: This prophecy would come to pass when Baasha rose to power in Israel and ended Jeroboam's line (see 1 Kings 15:27).

15. HE WILL UPROOT ISRAEL FROM THIS GOOD LAND: Ahijah announced God's judgment would fall on the nation of Israel for joining Jeroboam's apostasy. The people would be "struck" by the Lord and sway like a reed in a rushing river—a biblical metaphor for political instability (see Matthew 11:7; Luke 7:24).

16. HE WILL GIVE ISRAEL UP: The Lord was prophesying that He would one day uproot Israel from Palestinian soil and scatter it in exile east of the Euphrates River. This occurred nearly 100 years later when the Assyrians invaded

and led the people into captivity (see 2 Kings 17:22–23). Yet this was not a surprise to the Israelites, for the Lord had warned them He would do this if they chased after foreign gods (see Deuteronomy 28:63–64). Although Israel's idolatry would eventually lead them into captivity, the Lord never abandoned them. He does send discipline into the lives of His children, but He will never cast them away completely.

17. CAME TO TIRZAH: By this time Jeroboam had apparently moved his capital from Shechem to Tirzah, located in the tribal region of Manasseh, about seven miles northeast of Shechem and thirty-five miles north of Jerusalem. Tirzah was famous for its beauty. "O my love, you are as beautiful as Tirzah, lovely as Jerusalem, awesome as an army with banners!" (Song of Solomon 6:4).

20. TWENTY-TWO YEARS: Jeroboam reigned from 931 to 910 BC.

UNLEASHING THE TEXT

1) Why did Jeroboam send his wife to Ahijah instead of to one of the priests he had appointed? What does this reveal about his syncretistic beliefs?

_____

_____

_____

_____

2) Why did Jeroboam have his wife wear a disguise? What did he hope to accomplish? What does this reveal about his views of God?

_____

_____

_____

3) Why did the Lord allow Jeroboam's son to die? What does it mean that there was "something good toward the LORD" to be found in him (verse 13)?

_____

_____

_____

4) How did Jeroboam's sin differ from the sins of Solomon? How were they similar? In what ways did Solomon's sins open the door for the sin of Jeroboam?

_____

_____

_____

EXPLORING THE MEANING

Syncretism is a form of idolatry. Syncretism is the act of mixing together elements from different religions to create a sort of hybrid religious system. The process can refer to intermingling diverse religious practices, or it can refer to those who attempt to reconcile opposing viewpoints. Jeroboam committed the sin of syncretism when he attempted to mingle pagan idolatry with God's commanded worship. It is easy to see the idolatry of Jeroboam's acts, as he literally created two golden calves for the people to worship.

But syncretism is still idolatry even when it doesn't involve golden calves. The basic motivation behind syncretism is rebellion against God's Word. Individuals decide they want to worship God in their own way and reject certain aspects of Scripture in favor of their own ideas. This is the idolatry of self—making oneself to be equal with God and pushing the Lord into the background, just as Jeroboam did. The world continually encourages syncretism for the simple reason that it hates the teachings of Christ and does everything in its power to move believers away from God's Word. Many use the excuse that the gospel must be made "relevant" to our culture in order to ignore scriptural principles and add in principles that are not scriptural.

Such attempts to mix the teachings of the world with the doctrines of God's Word are syncretistic. The Bible is the final authority on how to approach God, and we do not have the privilege of rewriting Scripture to fit our own desires or to fit into the culture of the world around us. When cultural teachings and practices go against the teachings of the Bible, we are called to choose between the two—but not to attempt some compromise incorporating elements of both. We are called to choose once and for all to serve God, and to serve Him in His way, not in our own way. Anything else is idolatry.

Even non-believers call on God in times of trouble. Jeroboam is a fascinating case study on how those who reject God's authority still call on Him in times of trouble. Jeroboam made no secret of his disdain for God and His Word. He instituted his own priesthood, rejected the traditional Jewish holidays and replaced them with his own, and even built altars to gods whom he invented. In short, Jeroboam turned his back on God and replaced Him with his own religion.

But when Jeroboam's hand was withered, he immediately asked the prophet to pray for him (see 1 Kings 13:6). Again, when his son fell ill, he sent his wife to the prophet. Jeroboam's hypocrisy is so obvious it's startling, and it crystallizes the dilemma of those who reject God. On the one hand, Jeroboam invented his own religion and rejected the Lord of the universe. But on the other hand, his new religion was powerless to heal him or save his son. It is ironic when circumstances force the nonbeliever to outwardly call on God for help.

This kind of plea does not reflect a genuine desire to have a relationship with God. We see this in Jeroboam's life, for when God did heal his hand, it did not result in his repentance. It is naïve to think that had God also healed Jeroboam's son, he would have submitted his life to God's authority. Conversion comes when a person humbles himself and realizes that God is good and holy, while sinners are deserving of judgment. When a sinner cries to God for forgiveness, it is granted. When a nonbeliever cries to God in the face of a trial, God may or may not answer, as these cries are not indicative of true repentance.

The ultimate trial, of course, is death. When nonbelievers stand before God for judgment, there will be many who, like Jeroboam, will call out to the

Lord for help. Jesus said that in death there will be many who will say to Him, "Lord, Lord," but He will cast them away, because He never really knew them (see Matthew 7:22–23).

God's discipline is for our good. The people of Israel rebelled against the Lord, rejected His commands, and insisted on walking in their own ways. The nation's history was actually riddled with such rebellion, from the time the Israelites left Egypt right up to the time the Lord sent them into captivity. God continually showed Himself faithful and loving to His people—and they continually showed themselves to be rebellious.

This tendency is not unique to the nation of Israel. On the contrary, it is common to all humankind. We are all descendants of Adam, and we all possess Adam's fallen and rebellious nature. The Lord rebuked and disciplined Israel repeatedly throughout their history, and He will do the same to His children today. But we must remember that His discipline is as much a part of His loving faithfulness as is His blessing. All that He does in the lives of believers is designed for their benefit and intended to make them into the image of His Son, Jesus.

The Lord will never abandon His children. The day of judgment is indeed coming, and there will be many who will be cast out of God's presence— but those who are redeemed through the blood of Christ shall never be cast out. We may suffer hardship and discipline, for, as stated above, the Lord does discipline those whom He loves (see Hebrews 12:5–6), but no Christian needs to fear that God will abandon him. "The LORD . . . will not leave you nor forsake you" (Deuteronomy 31:8).

REFLECTING ON THE TEXT

5) Define *syncretism* in your own words. Why is it a sinful practice? Why does God view it as stinking garbage (see 1 Kings 14:10)?

_____

_____

_____

6) In what ways is syncretism a form of idolatry? What is idolatrous about it? What motivates a person to commit syncretism?

_____

_____

_____

_____

7) What is the difference between God's discipline and God's judgment? What is God's purpose when He sends discipline into our lives?

_____

_____

_____

_____

_____

8) What are some examples of syncretism that have crept into Christian teachings today? What does the Bible say about these teachings?

_____

_____

_____

_____

_____

PERSONAL RESPONSE

9) How do we know that Christians will never face judgment? Give evidence from the Scriptures.

_____

_____

_____

_____

10) In what ways have you allowed syncretism into your relationship with God? What will you do to remove worldly elements from your worship?

_____

_____

_____

_____

4

THE FIRST KINGS OF JUDAH
1 Kings 14:21–15:8

DRAWING NEAR

What are some things a leader must do to reestablish his confidence and authority after making a mistake? How can this process actually make him or her a better leader?

_____

_____

_____

THE CONTEXT

The kingdoms of Israel and Judah both suffered because of their unfaithfulness to God. They lost sight of their position as the Lord's chosen people, and ultimately, because of this, they lost their relationship with the Lord as well. As one king after another led the people into idolatry, the two kingdoms began to look and act exactly like their pagan neighbors.

As we have seen, God ripped Solomon's kingdom in two as a result of the idolatry during his reign. Jeroboam, king of Israel, led his people into a syncretistic mixture of Canaanite worship and worship of the one true God. Rehoboam, king of Judah, also led his people into the detestable practices of the Canaanite people, building high places for pagan worship and instituting ritual male prostitution. "They provoked [God] to jealousy with their sins which they committed, more than all that their fathers had done" (1 Kings 14:22).

In this study, we will see that God would not allow these sins to go unpunished. He allowed the armies of Shishak, king of Egypt, to invade Judah and strip the treasures in the temple and the royal palace. Along with the tensions with Egypt, there would also be continual warfare between Judah and Israel, and these tensions would extend into the reign of Abijam, Rehoboam's son. Yet God would still not forsake His promise of a king reigning on David's throne. Ultimately, Jesus would fill this role and fulfill God's promise to His people.

God will keep His promises, but He requires undivided hearts for His people to experience the blessing of those promises. He seeks hearts like that of David who, though he suffered because of sin, turned toward God in repentance. Unfortunately, most of the kings of Judah and Israel would not have hearts like this toward God.

KEYS TO THE TEXT

Read 1 Kings 14:21–15:8, noting the key words and phrases indicated below.

JUDAH UNDER REHOBOAM: Rehoboam takes the throne in Judah after the two kingdoms split. Like his father, Solomon, before him, he also leads the people into idolatry.

14:21. REHOBOAM THE SON OF SOLOMON: As we saw in a previous study, when Solomon drifted away from obedience to God's Word, the Lord had told him that He would tear the kingdom of Israel away from his descendants. However, God also said that He would leave one tribe under the authority of his son, Rehoboam, and that tribe would be Judah.

THE CITY WHICH THE LORD HAD CHOSEN: As we have seen, the Lord had commanded His people to worship Him at the city He had set apart, which was

Jerusalem (see Deuteronomy 12:1–14; 1 Kings 9:3). Jeroboam, Israel's first king, had set up idols and created new worship centers for the people—effectively replacing Jerusalem as the center of worship.

NAAMAH, AN AMMONITESS: Solomon had allowed his many pagan wives to lead him astray from following the Lord. It is possible that one such wife, Naamah, led him into the paganism of her Ammonite heritage (see 1 Kings 11:5). Whether or not she was influential in Solomon's idolatry, she undoubtedly had that effect on her son Rehoboam.

22. JUDAH DID EVIL: The author of Chronicles states that God's blessing rested on Rehoboam for three years because of the people's commitment to the Lord's ways. However, Rehoboam, like his father before him, took many wives and concubines, which led him to become disaffected toward the Lord (see 2 Chronicles 11:16–21). Judah under Rehoboam would end up outdoing her ancestors in evil and provoking the Lord to jealous anger.

23. HIGH PLACES, SACRED PILLARS, AND WOODEN IMAGES: The high places were heathen worship sites that the Canaanites had used prior to Israel's arrival in the Promised Land. The sacred pillars were stones that had been set up vertically and dedicated to some pagan deity, often with the god's name inscribed. The wooden images were probably "Asherah poles"—symbols of the goddess Asherah that were associated with the licentious practices of Canaanite nature religions. The Lord had expressly commanded His people to destroy all these elements of paganism when they arrived in Canaan (see Deuteronomy 12:2–4).

ON EVERY HIGH HILL AND UNDER EVERY GREEN TREE: This phrase is a quotation from Deuteronomy 12:2: "You shall utterly destroy all the places where the nations you shall dispossess served their gods, on the high mountains and on the hills and under every green tree." The author of 1 Kings may have been intentionally drawing his readers' attention to the fact that the worship practices of Israel and Judah were in direct contradiction to God's Word.

24. PERVERTED PERSONS IN THE LAND: These were male prostitutes who practiced wickedness at the pagan shrines in Canaan. Sexual license was an integral part of Canaanite nature religions, which taught that such practices would ensure a good harvest.

ALL THE ABOMINATIONS OF THE NATIONS: God had given the Promised Land to the Israelites because the Canaanites had engaged in wicked practices—yet now the Israelites were adopting those very same practices. The fact that Israel was God's chosen nation did not give them license to engage in such iniquity. On the contrary, the Lord held them to a higher standard because they were His chosen people. If the Lord had driven out the Canaanites for such sins, He would certainly also drive out the Israelites.

GOD'S PUNISHMENT ON JUDAH: God's judgment against the people of Judah comes in the form of an invasion from Egypt—the nation that had once held their ancestors in slavery.

25. SHISHAK KING OF EGYPT CAME UP AGAINST JERUSALEM: Presumably, Rehoboam's three years of blessing preceded a fourth year of spiritual rebellion, which God judged with an invasion at the hand of the Egyptians (c. 927/926 BC). The invading king was Shishak, founder of the twenty-second dynasty in Egypt, who reigned from 945–924 BC. An Egyptian record of this invasion stated that Shishak's army penetrated all the way north to the Sea of Galilee. He wanted to restore Egypt's once-great power, but he was unable to conquer both Israel and Judah.

26. HE TOOK AWAY THE TREASURES: Shishak was, however, able to destroy cities in Judah, gain some control of trade routes, and plunder the temple. The author of Chronicles writes that in the face of this Egyptian conqueror, the leaders of Judah humbled themselves and repented before God (see 2 Chronicles 12:1–8). This was the Israelites' first major military encounter with Egypt since the exodus, and it must have been bitter for them to again be enslaved to a people from whom God had liberated them.

27. KING REHOBOAM MADE BRONZE SHIELDS IN THEIR PLACE: These were ceremonial shields crafted in Solomon's day and used as part of the "dress uniform" of the palace guards (the shields used in battle were generally reinforced with iron, which is much harder than bronze but not as attractive). Rehoboam gave these shields to Shishak as ransom and replaced them with bronze shields. The decline from gold to bronze is quite telling regarding Judah's spiritual condition: bronze shines like gold, but it is only a cheap imitation.

29. THE REST OF THE ACTS OF REHOBOAM: The author of Chronicles states that when the people of Judah repented, God turned His wrath from them and spared the nation (see 2 Chronicles 12:12–14). Rehoboam's reign

acquired new life and continued on for many years, but he ultimately faltered and did evil in the sight of the Lord.

30. WAR BETWEEN REHOBOAM AND JEROBOAM: Many border skirmishes ensued as the armies in the north and south maneuvered for tactical advantage and control of territory.

ABIJAM TAKES THE THRONE: Reboboam's son Abijam takes the throne after his father's death and continues his father's idolatry.

15:1. ABIJAM: He was the son of Rehoboam. In 2 Chronicles 13:1–2 we read that he was first called "Abijah." Because Abijam means "father of the sea" and Abijah means "my father is the LORD," he might have had his name changed because of his sin.

2. MAACHAH THE GRANDDAUGHTER OF ABISHALOM: Abishalom may refer to Absalom, King David's son. Abijam, therefore, would be David's great-great-grandson.

3. THE HEART OF HIS FATHER DAVID: David was a man after God's own heart (see 1 Samuel 13:14), which means he strove all his life to walk in obedience to God's Word. Rehoboam, by contrast, had walked according to the desires of the flesh, and that had led him to do great wickedness. The kings of Judah were generally categorized as either walking as David had walked or walking in the sins of their fathers.

4. FOR DAVID'S SAKE: The Lord had promised King David that his heirs would always occupy the throne in Jerusalem (see 2 Samuel 7:12–16). This promise was ultimately fulfilled in the person of Christ, whose kingdom is established forever.

5. DAVID DID WHAT WAS RIGHT IN THE EYES OF THE LORD: David's life was characterized by obedience to God's commands and by a desire to walk faithfully with the Lord. The "matter of Uriah the Hittite" refers to David's adultery with Bathsheba and murder of her husband, Uriah. This grievous sin brought lasting consequences to David's family, yet even at that time David demonstrated his desire to serve God by repenting when confronted by the prophet Nathan.

6. THERE WAS WAR BETWEEN REHOBOAM AND JEROBOAM: That is, between the house of Rehoboam and Jeroboam. Abijam's father, Rehoboam, was dead by this time.

GOING DEEPER

Read 2 Chronicles 13:1-21, noting the key words and phrases indicated below.

ANOTHER SIDE OF ABIJAM: The author of Chronicles sheds some additional light on the life of Abijam and reveals that he was not entirely given over to evil.

1. ABIJAH BECAME KING: Abijah/Abijam would reign in Judah for three years, from 913-911 BC.

3. FOUR HUNDRED THOUSAND CHOICE MEN ... EIGHT HUNDRED THOUSAND CHOICE MEN: These numbers are large but not surprising given the immense number of capable men who could fight, as counted in David's census (see 1 Chronicles 21:5). This was no small skirmish but open war between Judah and Israel. In this we see the severe repercussions of sin in the descendants of Jacob. The nation had been divided into two separate kingdoms, and now God's chosen people were trying to destroy one another.

4. MOUNT ZEMARAIM: The exact location is uncertain, but this was probably just north of the boundary between Israel and Judah, near Bethel.

5. COVENANT OF SALT: Salt is associated elsewhere with the Mosaic covenant sacrifices (see Leviticus 2:13), the priestly covenant (see Numbers 18:19), and the New Covenant symbolic sacrifices in the millennial kingdom (see Ezekiel 43:24). The preservative quality of salt represents the fidelity or loyalty intended in keeping the covenant. Here, it would refer to God's irrevocable pledge and intended loyalty in fulfilling the Davidic covenant.

6. JEROBOAM . . . ROSE AND REBELLED AGAINST HIS LORD: Abijam failed to mention that the Lord had actually ordained Jeroboam to become king over Israel.

7. REHOBOAM WAS YOUNG AND INEXPERIENCED: As noted previously, it was Rehoboam's foolishness that had led to the division of the kingdom.

8. KINGDOM OF THE LORD: Abijam reminded the people that the Davidic covenant represented God's expressed will about who would rule on His behalf in the earthly kingdom. Judah was thus God's nation because the king was in the line of David.

9. CAST OUT THE PRIESTS OF THE LORD: As we saw in an earlier study, Jeroboam had replaced God's ordained priesthood, the sons of Aaron, with

anyone he chose. He had also told the people that they were free to worship God at various centers he had appointed, each with its own golden calf, rather than make the journey to Jerusalem as the Lord had commanded.

10. THE LORD IS OUR GOD: Abijam professed a commitment on behalf of the nation of Judah to only worship the one true God.

11. YOU HAVE FORSAKEN HIM: Abijam's assessment was accurate at this point: to create one's own form of religion is to forsake the Lord. Those who want to walk faithfully with the Lord will obey His commands and avoid the temptation to ignore some parts of His Word or add their own rules and regulations to it.

CIVIL WAR: Jeroboam disregards Abijam's counsel and sets up an ambush. Abijam and the army of Judah call on the Lord, and He gives them the victory.

14. THEY CRIED OUT TO THE LORD: The army of Israel was expecting some golden idols to give them victory, while Judah's army cried out to the Lord for protection. The results speak for themselves. The Lord is always faithful to guide and protect those who call out to Him.

15. GOD STRUCK JEROBOAM AND ALL ISRAEL: The army of Judah was surrounded, with 400,000 enemy troops behind them and the same number in front, and their defeat was certain. It is unknown what God did to intervene, but the army of Israel began to flee.

17. FIVE HUNDRED THOUSAND CHOICE MEN OF ISRAEL FELL SLAIN: The battle represented both a victory and a great tragedy. The Lord had shown Himself faithful to Judah and had demonstrated that He alone can give victory. Yet His chosen nation had been divided against itself, with brother taking up arms against brother. This was not His desire.

19. TOOK CITIES FROM HIM: The city of Bethel was located twelve miles north of Jerusalem. The locations of Jeshanah and Ephrain are not known, but they are believed to be in the vicinity of Bethel.

20. THE LORD STRUCK HIM: God again intervened, in a manner not described, to end the life of the wicked king Jeroboam (c. 910 BC).

21. ABIJAH GREW MIGHTY: Before the battle, Jeroboam outnumbered Abijam two to one; after the battle, Abijam outnumbered Jeroboam four to three. Abijam's reign would be characterized by some good and some wickedness.

Like Solomon before him, he did not serve the Lord wholeheartedly: "His heart was not loyal to the LORD his God, as was the heart of his father David" (1 Kings 11:4).

UNLEASHING THE TEXT

1) From what you know about Rehoboam, what opportunities did he have to know God and obey His word? What influences did he have that might have pulled him away from God?

---

2) What does it mean that the people of Judah provoked God "to jealousy with their sins" (1 Kings 12:22)? What does God's response reveal about the magnitude of this sin? What does the sin of idol worship say about the state of the king's and the people's hearts?

---

3) What consequences did Judah experience because of its sin? What was God's purpose in allowing His people to suffer these consequences?

---

4) In what way was Abijam different than his father? In what way was he the same? How would you summarize his reign over Judah?

_____

_____

_____

EXPLORING THE MEANING

The Lord always keeps His promises. The Lord promised David that his descendants would sit on the throne in Jerusalem and that his throne would be established forever. Further, the Lord assured David that He would be a father to Solomon and "chasten him with the rod of men" (2 Samuel 7:14) if Solomon fell into sin. When this happened, God kept His promise and disciplined Solomon by tearing away most of the kingdom from his son Rehoboam. Yet at the same time, the Lord kept His promise by allowing Judah to retain the line of David.

Similarly, the Lord swore to Jeroboam that his descendants would sit on the throne of Israel as long as Jeroboam obeyed God's commands and walked faithfully according to His Word (see 1 Kings 13:8). The implication of this promise was that the Lord would *not* establish Jeroboam's throne if he did *not* walk in faithfulness—and that, unfortunately, is how it turned out. Jeroboam led the northern tribes into idolatry, and the Lord removed him from the throne, just as He promised He would.

In keeping His promises to David and Jeroboam, the Lord established the Messianic line in Judah. Jeroboam's idolatry made it clear that true Messianic hope could only be found in a descendent of David, and as long as Judah existed, there was a descendent of David as her king. Even though Judah was removed from the land, God's promise to David was eventually realized in Jesus, a descendant of David, who reigns in heaven over His people now and forevermore.

The world's idols cannot save. Jeroboam had established golden calves to serve as the focus of the Israelites' worship. His intention was to draw the people away from worshiping the Lord at the temple in Jerusalem. In doing so, he was attempting to solidify the split between the twelve tribes. But Jeroboam's plan had larger ramifications: some years later, Israel's army carried those golden calves into battle, placing their faith in man-made idols for victory.

Abijam, by contrast, openly declared that God was at the head of Judah's army and placed his trust in the Lord. That trust was not misplaced, for the Lord quickly vindicated the army of Judah by miraculously intervening on their behalf and routing the army of Israel. Indeed, the entire conflict might have been avoided if Israel had turned away from their golden calves and heeded the sound advice that Abijam offered.

The world today still urges us to place our faith in false idols such as wealth, prestige, or self-reliance. Yet these things are no more effective than a statue of a cow. The devil does not care in what we place our faith, as long as it is not the God who created us. But the fact is that idols are powerless to rescue us from our troubles.

The Lord is in control, even when His people are foolish. Even during Solomon's life the Lord had declared that the unified nation of Israel would be split into two. God had told Jeroboam he would rule ten of the tribes, which revealed the consequences of Solomon's sin. The Lord would not allow His people to prosper and be blessed while they were pursuing other gods.

However, notice the way in which the Lord allowed the division to happen. Rehoboam was foolish and rejected the wise counsel of his father's advisors while listening to the brash counsel of his friends. Meanwhile, Jeroboam was establishing calves as centers of worship, marking a permanent break between Israel and Judah. Rehoboam's foolishness and Jeroboam's idolatry were both sinful, but they were also the means by which the Lord fulfilled His prophecy that the kingdom would be divided.

It is important for us to understand that God is in control even when the world seems out of control. In fact, God often uses sin and its effects to bring about His perfect plan. No event in Scripture illustrates this truth as well as the betrayal and crucifixion of Jesus. Pilate was judged for betraying the Prince of Life, but Jesus said that Pilate only had the power to do what God had ordained (see John 19:11). Similarly, Judas was judged for betraying Jesus, but this sinful act of betrayal was what led to the death of Christ and the consummation of God's plan of salvation. Of course, this never excuses sin, but it does assure us that God is in charge of all things, and that all things are working for His glory (see Romans 11:36).

REFLECTING ON THE TEXT

5) Why does God demand moral purity in His followers? How does immorality affect Christians' influence on others? How does it affect their relationship with God?

_____

_____

_____

_____

6) How does understanding God's sovereignty give us confidence in the midst of chaotic and sinful times?

_____

_____

_____

7) What idols and false gods do people tend to follow today? Why do so many people tend to place their faith them? How do such things fail in the end?

_____

_____

_____

8) What promises have you seen God fulfill in your life? What promises do you rely on when facing trials or temptation?

_____

_____

_____

PERSONAL RESPONSE

9) Are there any idols in your life? Are you placing your trust in something other than God? What must you do to rid your life of those idols?

_____

_____

_____

10) Are there any areas of impurity in your life? What will you do this week to remove them?

_____

_____

_____

5

THE KINGSHIP OF ASA
1 Kings 15:9–24

DRAWING NEAR

In what ways does the world tend to discredit people or hold them in esteem based on their family or their upbringing? What does God look at when it comes to evaluating a person?

_____

_____

_____

THE CONTEXT

King Abijam reigned in Judah for only three years. He was not a godly king, and he led the nation of Judah into idolatry and wickedness, just as his father, Rehoboam, had done before him. As we have already seen, this trend dated back to the reign of Solomon, Abijam's grandfather. Thus far in Judah's history, the old saying had held true: "like father, like son."

Given this, we would not have expectations that anything would be different when Abijam's son Asa took the throne. After all, three previous generations had led God's people into idol worship, so it would only be reasonable to expect the same from the new king. However, as we have seen, the Lord is not constrained by a person's lineage and family background. He can choose to use anyone to further His purposes and plans on the earth, no matter how unlikely a candidate that person might seem.

Even though King Asa came from a family of compromisers, he turned his heart toward God and strove to follow His Word. As a result, the Lord used him to lead Judah away from idolatry and back toward Himself. However, once again we find a king who was only partially obedient to God, for though Asa tore down the pagan high places, he only tore down some of them. This tendency of holding back on obedience would later come back to betray the king, and he would finish his days with a heart that was hardened to the Lord.

Nevertheless, Asa is defined in Scripture as a good king—a leader who did what was right in the eyes of the Lord.

KEYS TO THE TEXT

Read 1 Kings 15:9–24, noting the key words and phrases indicated below.

> *KING ASA PURGES FALSE WORSHIP: When Asa takes the throne, he reverses the policies of the kings before him and leads to the people to walk in obedience to God's Word.*

9. ASA BECAME KING OVER JUDAH: Asa, the son of Abijam, would rule over Judah for forty-one years (c. 911–870 BC). He enacted four policies that made him a godly king: (1) he removed the "sacred" prostitutes from Judah; (2) he rid the land of idols; (3) he removed the corrupt queen mother from power and burned the idol she had made; and (4) he placed "holy things" (items he and his father had dedicated to the Lord) back in the temple.

13. QUEEN MOTHER: Maachah was Asa's grandmother, and she held a place of honor within the king's court. Her functions would have included being an advisor to the king and a teacher of the king's children. In these capacities, she would have exerted a profound influence over national policies and the future kings of Judah.

AN OBSCENE IMAGE OF ASHERAH: The term *obscene* is derived from a Hebrew verb that means "to shudder" (see Job 9:6). It suggests the idol Maachah had installed was shocking, perhaps even sexually explicit, in nature. Asa burned the idol near Brook Kidron, a seasonal river that ran through the Kidron Valley at the eastern boundary of Jerusalem.

14. THE HIGH PLACES WERE NOT REMOVED: Some of these high places were devoted to idolatry, while others were used for a syncretistic blending of paganism with the true worship of God. Asa evidently failed to remove those that blended paganism and truth. In this way, Asa obeyed the Lord for the most part but stopped short of complete obedience. Toward the end of his life, this inclination would cause him problems.

WAR WITH ISRAEL: *Once again, the nation of Israel attempts to besiege Judah. Asa's tactics in defending his country prove to be unwise.*

16. BAASHA KING OF ISRAEL: Judah enjoyed ten years of peace after Asa's father, Abijam, defeated Jeroboam and the army of Israel. After Jeroboam's death, his son Nadab rules for only two years before a man named Baasha rose up and overthrew him (see 1 Kings 15:25–34). Baasha then renewed the war between Israel and Judah.

17. CAME UP AGAINST JUDAH: The author of Chronicles states this battle took place "in the thirty-sixth year of the reign of Asa" (2 Chronicles 16:1). Since King Baasha died in the twenty-sixth year of Asa's reign (see 1 Kings 15:33), this could not mean Judah and Israel were at war ten years later. However, if the time reference were to the thirty-fifth year *since the kingdom was divided*, it would put the year at c. 896 BC, during the fourteenth year of Baasha's reign and the sixteenth of Asa's reign. The book of the record of the kings of Judah and Israel, from which the writer drew his account, generally followed this manner of reckoning.

17. BUILT RAMAH: King Baasha built this city on the border between Judah and Israel, just north of Jerusalem. It was situated on a major highway and served to blockade Jerusalem.

18. ASA TOOK ALL THE SILVER AND GOLD: Asa raided the treasuries of Judah and sent a sizable gift to Ben-Hadad I, ruler of the Syrian kingdom, to influence him to break his treaty with Israel. The majority of historians

believe Ben-Hadad I reigned from c. 900–860 BC and was succeeded by a son or grandson, Ben-Hadad II, who ruled c. 860–841 BC.

19. LET THERE BE A TREATY BETWEEN YOU AND ME: Asa was hoping the gift would influence Ben-Hadad I to also enter into a treaty with Judah so they could invade Israel from the north. This initially appeared to be a successful political move on Asa's part, but the king's quickness to negotiate rather than pray and seek deliverance displeased the Lord. The author of Chronicles notes there had also been a treaty between his father, Abijam, and Tabrimmon, the father of Ben-Hadad I and former king of Syria (see 2 Chronicles 16:3).

20. THE CITIES OF ISRAEL: The army of Ben-Hadad I invaded Israel and took cities to the north of the Sea of Galilee. This conquest gave Syria control of the trade routes to the Mediterranean coast and Israel's fertile Jezreel Valley, and it also made Syria a great military threat to Israel. (See the gray area on the map in the Introduction for an approximate outline of what was taken by Syria.) Baasha wisely gave up fortifying Ramah and went to live in Tirzah, the capital of Israel.

22. KING ASA BUILT GEBA . . . AND MIZPAH: When the Israelite army withdrew, Asa conscripted a Judean labor force to dismantle his enemy's work and reuse the materials for fortifications against them. Again, from a human perspective, Asa's strategy was shrewd—but the problem was that he depended on Syria rather than the Lord to rescue him.

GOING DEEPER

The author of Chronicles gives us some additional details about Asa's reign not found in the book of Kings. Read 2 Chronicles 14:2–16, noting the key words and phrases indicated below.

ASA'S FAITHFUL YEARS: The author of Chronicles reveals that most of Asa's reign was characterized by a devotion to God's commands, which made him one of Judah's good kings.

14:2. ASA DID WHAT WAS GOOD AND RIGHT: These events took place prior to Asa's battle against Baasha of Israel and his subsequent treaty with Syria in 1 Kings 15:16–21.

4. HE COMMANDED JUDAH: Asa understood the role of God's anointed king, which was to lead the people into obedience to God's commands. Too many of Judah's kings did just the opposite, leading God's people into idolatry through their own disobedience. Asa knew that a godly king must lead his subjects by example. He was not perfect, but for the most part he walked in faithfulness to God, and the people followed.

SEEK THE LORD . . . OBSERVE THE LAW: Notice the deliberate actions that are required of God's people. *Seeking* involves an intense search for something, while *observing* involves paying attention to something once it is found. Christians are called to seek the Lord and search diligently in His Word for an understanding of His character and will. We are also called to observe and pay attention to His ways as we grow in understanding and maturity. We must also observe our own lives regularly and be on guard to ensure that we are walking faithfully.

EGYPT ATTACKS: Egypt sends an army of mercenaries to attack Judah, but Asa responds wisely by crying out to the Lord for help.

8. ASA HAD AN ARMY: Notice the equipment listed for Asa's army did not include chariots. The army from Ethiopia, by contrast, had some 300. Chariots in ancient battle were equivalent to modern tanks and were superior in combat against foot soldiers. Asa's army may have outnumbered the Ethiopians, but they were outmatched by the enemy's weaponry.

9. THEN ZERAH THE ETHIOPIAN CAME OUT AGAINST THEM: Zerah was likely invading Judah on behalf of the Egyptian Pharaoh, who was attempting to regain control of the region as Shishak had during the days of Rehoboam.

10. VALLEY OF ZEPHATHAH AT MARESHAH: The city of Mareshah was located about eight miles southeast of Gath and twenty-five miles southwest of Jerusalem. Rehoboam had earlier reinforced this city.

11. IT IS NOTHING FOR YOU TO HELP: Asa's appeal to God centered on the Lord's omnipotence and reputation. Asa recognized the Lord could defeat a massive army just as easily as if they were a handful of children. What mattered was not the strength of the foe but God's ability to answer prayer.

13. THEY WERE BROKEN BEFORE THE LORD: The Lord not only gave Judah victory over her enemies but also utterly broke their power. Egypt would not become a world power again for another 150 years.

Read 2 Chronicles 16:7–14, noting the key words and phrases indicated below.

KING ASA's LATER YEARS: The author of Chronicles notes that during Asa's battle with Baasha, the Lord sent a prophet to confront him about his treaty with Syria, but Asa did not repent.

16:7. HANANI THE SEER: God used this prophet to (1) rebuke Asa for his wicked appropriation of temple treasures devoted to God to purchase power, and (2) to rebuke him for his faithless dependence on a pagan king instead of the Lord.

NOT RELIED ON THE LORD YOUR GOD: Asa's strategy of bringing the Syrian army in behind his enemy was brilliant from a military perspective, but it showed a lack of trust in God. Asa had placed his faith in Syria's army and did not act as if the Lord was the leader of Judah's army. The king had seen God's miraculous deliverance against the forces of Egypt and Ethiopia, and he should have called on the Lord to deliver him from the army of Israel as well.

SYRIA HAS ESCAPED FROM YOUR HAND: The Lord would have given Asa victory over the nation of Syria as well as Israel if he had cried out to Him on this occasion. As a result, the nation of Syria would remain Judah's enemy for a long time to come.

9. THE EYES OF THE LORD: Christians should always be seeking the Lord, but it is comforting to know the Lord is always seeking those who are willing to be used by Him. He seeks those who are lost to bring them to salvation (see Luke 19:10), and He seeks opportunities to show His power and blessings to those who serve Him.

10. ASA WAS ANGRY WITH THE SEER: Sadly, King Asa's heart seems to have grown hard toward the Lord and His commands, and he took out his anger on the Lord's prophet. At some point in his life, Asa evidently began to place his trust in men and armies rather than in the Lord who alone gives victory. His anger at God's prophet contrasts sharply with King David, who repented of his sin the moment Nathan confronted him (see 2 Samuel 12).

A SAD ENDING: During Asa's last six years, he exhibits the ungodly behavior of anger at the truth, oppression of God's people, and seeking the aid of humans instead of God.

12. IN THE THIRTY-NINTH YEAR OF HIS REIGN: Asa would die as a result of what may have been severe gangrene (c. 870 BC).

HE DID NOT SEEK THE LORD, BUT THE PHYSICIANS: Asa continued to place his faith in the power and learning of men rather than in the Lord. This does not mean it is wrong to seek medical help from doctors, but it does remind us that healing comes only from God. One should rely on the Lord for healing even while seeking human medical attention.

14. MADE A VERY GREAT BURNING: Although the Hebrews rarely employed cremation, the people honored Asa for his long reign and notable accomplishments with this memorial at his death. Later, King Jehoram would not be honored by fire in the same way because of his shameful reign (see 1 Kings 21:19).

UNLEASHING THE TEXT

1) Why did Asa remove his grandmother from her position as queen mother? What influence did she have? What did he gain by removing her?

_____

_____

_____

_____

2) Why would Asa have removed only some of the high places? What might have motivated him to keep some? How might this apply in your own life?

_____

_____

_____

_____

3) How did Asa's reign as king compare with that of his father, Abijam? How were the two kings different? What resulted from each man's reign?

_____

_____

_____

4) Why did King Asa command the nation of Judah to seek God? What made this command effective? What made him a godly leader?

_____

_____

_____

EXPLORING THE MEANING

Place your trust in God, not in man. The author of Chronicles states that King Asa began his reign with an early conflict against an overwhelming foe. The army from Ethiopia numbered many times more than the forces of Judah and was far better equipped. They evidently were fighting on behalf of Pharaoh—and the people of Judah could well remember the defeat they had suffered the last time Egypt had invaded. But King Asa did not lose heart. He knew the world's most powerful army could not stand before the hand of God, and in that hour Asa placed his trust openly in God.

Unfortunately, over the years Asa came to place more faith in humans than he did in God. When King Baasha of Israel later invaded, Asa turned to the powerful nation of Syria to the north instead of turning to God as he had done before. This was in spite of the fact that the Israelites were a far less daunting foe than the Egyptians, and in spite of the fact that Syria was an ungodly nation. When Asa's health failed, he put his trust completely in the learning of men, preferring to turn to human doctors rather than the God who created him.

King Asa should have been warned by the Scripture, "Do not put your trust in princes, nor in a son of man, in whom there is no help" (Psalm 146:3). The physicians could not cure him, and Syria proved to be a treacherous ally, but God was always faithful. As the psalmist wrote, "The LORD is on my side, I will not fear. What can man do to me? . . . It is better to trust in the LORD than to put confidence in man" (Psalm 118:6, 8).

The godly leader leads by example. During the early years of King Asa's reign, he was a good leader for God's people because he ruled by example more than by command. It is true that he commanded the people of Judah to seek the Lord and to obey His precepts, but he first set the example by doing it himself. He turned away from the idolatry of his predecessors and removed the sites where such pagan practices took place. When he was faced with an overwhelming enemy during those early years, he turned to the Lord for protection rather than trusting in the power of his army or in alliances with others.

David was another king who led by example rather than by command. David's heart was always turned toward the Lord, and he strove throughout his life to be faithful to God's Word. When he did fall into sin, he was quick to repent when a prophet of God confronted him—which was contrary to Asa's response in his later years. Under David, the people could look to their king for an example of how to lead a godly life. This was exactly what God intended.

The New Testament teaches the same principle for all those who are in authority. Husbands are called to love their wives as Christ loved the church (see Ephesians 5:25). Elders are called to lead their flock by living as Jesus lived (see 1 Timothy 3:1–7). Older men and women are called to live godly lives so that those who are younger might learn by their examples (see Titus 2:1–5). In fact, each of us is called to live out the principles of Scripture, regardless of our situations in life, so that we might be a living testimony to the world around us of what it means to be a follower of Christ.

Christians must strive to finish the race well. King Asa started out strong. He had a heart for God and strove to obey His commands. He trusted fully in the Lord, even when the circumstances seemed overwhelming. Unfortunately, as we have seen, he did not finish his reign as he had begun. By the end of his life, he had turned his heart away from trusting the Lord, preferring to place his faith in the wisdom and power of men.

King Solomon followed the same pattern. He began his reign as a young man who called out to God for wisdom. He built the temple in response to God's command and led the people to follow the ways of the Lord. But as time went along, Solomon turned away from obedience and toward idolatry. Both Solomon and Asa did not *persevere* in maintaining godliness and purity, and the results were tragic. Nothing is quite as sad as watching a man begin his life strong in his commitment to God only to sink into worldliness and sin as time goes along.

Paul recognized this tendency in human nature to lose one's focus. He strove to maintain a strong discipline over the flesh, guarding against those snares and temptations that can gradually lure a person away from God's Word. He wrote, "Do you not know that those who run in a race all run, but one receives the prize? Run in such a way that you may obtain it. And everyone who competes for the prize is temperate in all things. Now they do it to obtain a perishable crown, but we for an imperishable crown" 1 Corinthians 9:24–25). The wise Christian will always remember to continue in spiritual training, staying the course for the long haul and striving to finish well.

REFLECTING ON THE TEXT

5) What happened in Asa's later years? What might have caused him to move away from faith in God? How might this principle apply in your own life?

_____

_____

_____

6) Why did Asa make a treaty with Syria rather than turning to God as he had done before? How might this have affected his attitude in later years?

_____

_____

_____

7) What is involved in seeking God? What is involved in observing His commands? Give some practical steps for doing each.

_____

_____

_____

8) What does it mean to rest on God (see 2 Chronicles 14:11)?

_____

_____

_____

PERSONAL RESPONSE

9) How well are you running the Christian race at present? What can you do this week to ensure that you finish the race well?

_____

_____

_____

10) When times of crisis come, where do you instinctively turn for help? Do you generally place your trust more in God or in people? Explain.

_____

_____

_____

THE MINISTRY OF ELIJAH

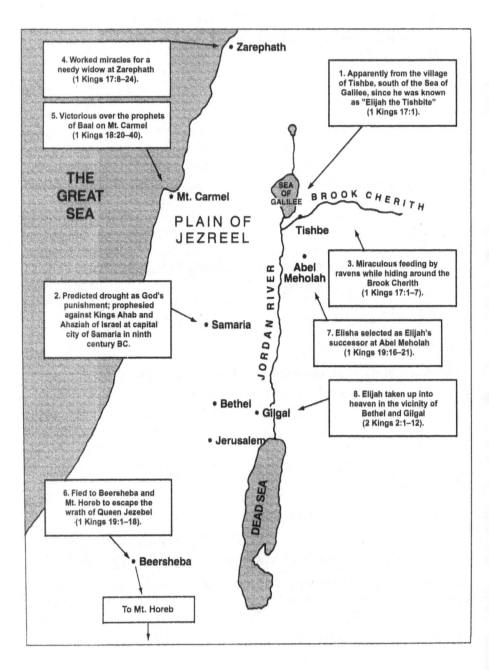

• Zarephath

4. Worked miracles for a needy widow at Zarephath (1 Kings 17:8–24).

1. Apparently from the village of Tishbe, south of the Sea of Galilee, since he was known as "Elijah the Tishbite" (1 Kings 17:1).

5. Victorious over the prophets of Baal on Mt. Carmel (1 Kings 18:20–40).

THE GREAT SEA

• Mt. Carmel

SEA OF GALILEE

BROOK CHERITH

PLAIN OF JEZREEL

Tishbe

• Abel Meholah

3. Miraculous feeding by ravens while hiding around the Brook Cherith (1 Kings 17:1–7).

2. Predicted drought as God's punishment; prophesied against Kings Ahab and Ahaziah of Israel at capital city of Samaria in ninth century BC.

• Samaria

JORDAN RIVER

7. Elisha selected as Elijah's successor at Abel Meholah (1 Kings 19:16–21).

• Bethel
• Gilgal

8. Elijah taken up into heaven in the vicinity of Bethel and Gilgal (2 Kings 2:1–12).

• Jerusalem

6. Fled to Beersheba and Mt. Horeb to escape the wrath of Queen Jezebel (1 Kings 19:1–18).

DEAD SEA

• Beersheba

To Mt. Horeb

6

THE KINGSHIP OF AHAB

1 Kings 16:1–17:7

DRAWING NEAR

How does our culture tend to define a "strong" leader? What types of characteristics do people tend to look for in choosing a person to lead them?

_____

_____

_____

THE CONTEXT

After Jeroboam, Israel had five different kings in quick succession, and each of them did evil in the sight of the Lord. Most of these kings followed Jeroboam's example by attempting to mix the worship of pagan gods with the worship of the Lord. This parade of wicked kings turned Israel into a pagan nation—one in which the worship of the true God was almost non-existent. But despite the wickedness of these kings, the worst for Israel was still ahead.

King Ahab, who came to power fifty years after Jeroboam's death, would give Israel a new standard for wickedness. Ahab's father, Omri, had purchased a hill northwest of Shechem and built a city there named Samaria. Ahab made this his capital and added a temple to it. That temple, however, was dedicated not to the worship of the Lord but to a heathen god named Baal, whom the Canaanites believed was responsible for sending rain and fruitful harvests. Ahab turned his heart fully to Baal worship and led the entire nation into pagan practices.

Ahab's wife was Jezebel—a name that has become synonymous with wickedness and treachery. She was the daughter of a Canaanite king and was also a priestess to Baal. As we read more about her personality in the book of 1 Kings, we will not find it surprising that Ahab followed her lead, for she was a woman who knew how to take charge and get things done.

The things that "got done" during Ahab's reign, however, were exceedingly wicked. Yet even in the midst of such wickedness, the Lord sent His people a prophet to give them another chance to turn back to Him. It was up to the people of Israel as to how they would respond.

KEYS TO THE TEXT

Read 1 Kings 16:1–17:7, noting the key words and phrases indicated below.

JUDGMENT AGAINST BAASHA: King Baasha, like his predecessors, does not follow the ways of the Lord, so God sends a prophet to inform him that his line will come to an end.

16:1. JEHU THE SON OF HANANI: This Hanani may have been the prophet who warned Judah's King Asa in 2 Chronicles 16:7–9. Jehu, like Ahijah before him, delivered the Lord's message of judgment to the king of Israel. The pattern that emerges in the book of Kings is the Lord using His prophets as a legitimate means by which to confront the sin of Israel's kings.

2. YOU HAVE WALKED IN THE WAY OF JEROBOAM: King Baasha had angered the Lord by following the sinful paths of Jeroboam. Appropriately, he faced the same humiliating judgment that Jeroboam had faced (see 1 Kings 14:10–11). Although he had waded through slaughter to get his throne, he still owed it to the permission of God, by whom all kings reign.

3. I WILL TAKE AWAY THE POSTERITY OF BAASHA: God's judgment against Baasha was that no long line of heirs would succeed him. Instead, his

family would be totally annihilated and their corpses shamefully scavenged by hungry dogs and birds.

8. ELAH . . . REIGNED TWO YEARS: Baasha's son Elah would reign only two years (c. 886–885 BC) before being overthrown by Zimri, the commander of the king's chariots. Zimri would end Elah's life when he was engaged in a binge of drinking at his steward Arza's house.

11. HE KILLED ALL THE HOUSEHOLD OF BAASHA: The words of Jehu the prophet thus came to pass when Zimri killed not only Elah but also his immediate sons. Zimri even went so far as to kill all of the extended relatives of Baasha who could potentially help his family.

OMRI COMES TO POWER: The death of Baasha sparks a power struggle that only comes to an end when Omri, a commander in Israel's army, is able to seize complete control of the throne.

15. ZIMRI HAD REIGNED IN TIRZAH SEVEN DAYS: Zimri's reign of seven days (c. 885 BC) would prove to be the shortest of any king of Israel. He was overthrown while the forces of Israel were encamped at Gibbethon, a city located about thirty-two miles west of Jerusalem. This city, which was situated in the territory of Dan, had been given to the Levites (see Joshua 19:44) but was now controlled by the Philistines, on whose border it lay.

16. OMRI . . . KING OVER ISRAEL: When the soldiers in the field heard of Elah's death, they acclaimed Omri, the commander of Israel's army, as the new king. Nothing is mentioned in the Bible about Omri's lineage, but the fact that his name is either Amorite or Arabic suggests he might have been a foreign mercenary. Although the author of Kings dedicates only a few verses to Omri, summing him up as one who did "evil in the eyes of the LORD" (verse 25), he was politically a powerful king who established the second longest dynasty in Israel.

21. HALF THE PEOPLE FOLLOWED TIBNI: Zimri's death automatically placed the kingdom of Israel in Omri's hands. Half of the population, including the army, then sided with Omri, but the other half backed a man named Tibni. Nothing further is known about him, but he was evidently strong enough to rival Omri for about four years.

22. THE PEOPLE WHO FOLLOWED OMRI PREVAILED: The coming of the dynasty of Omri to the kingship of Israel brought with it the introduction

of Baal worship with official sanction in Israel. Through intermarriage with the house of Omri, Baal worship penetrated into Judah and corrupted the line of David, initiating a gigantic struggle before Baalism was officially eradicated in both Israel and Judah.

23. OMRI . . . REIGNED TWELVE YEARS: Omri ruled twelve years (c. 885–874 BC), from Asa's twenty-seventh year to Asa's thirty-eighth year. This notice of his beginning to reign in Asa's thirty-first year must be a reference to his sole rule.

24. HE BOUGHT THE HILL OF SAMARIA: This hill, named after its owner, Shemer, was located seven miles northwest of Shechem and stood 300 feet high. Although it was ringed by other mountains, it stood by itself so that attackers had to charge uphill from every side. This new capital amounted to the northern equivalent of Jerusalem.

AHAB AND JEZEBEL: The royal crown has been passed six times since Jeroboam's rule, with each new king doing evil in the sight of the Lord. But Ahab and Jezebel will outdo them all.

16:29. AHAB THE SON OF OMRI: Five kings ruled Israel after Jeroboam, but Ahab would prove to be one of the wickedest in Israel's history. He would ultimately rule for twenty-two years (c. 874–853 BC). He ruled from his new capital in Samaria—a location that was convenient for everyone in Israel. In time the people of the city became known as *Samaritans*, and they figure in many Gospel passages of the New Testament.

30. AHAB . . . DID EVIL IN THE SIGHT OF THE LORD: This somber statement summarizes each of the preceding kings, as well, all the way back to Jeroboam. But with Ahab, Israel's spiritual decay reached its lowest point. He was even worse than his father, Omri, who was more wicked than all before him (see verse 25). Ahab's evil consisted of perpetuating all the sins of Jeroboam and promoting the worship of Baal in Israel.

31. AS THOUGH IT HAD BEEN A TRIVIAL THING: Jeroboam had established a precedent for the kings of Israel when he instituted idolatry, and his successors followed in his footsteps. But Ahab considered those sins to be normal, and that attitude led him even deeper into sin.

JEZEBEL THE DAUGHTER OF ETHBAAL: Jezebel's father, whose name meant "Baal is alive" was the king of Phoenicia (including Tyre and Sidon). He had murdered his predecessor and, according to Josephus, was a priest of the gods Melqart and Astarte. Jezebel herself was a priestess of Baal, and in the Bible she is portrayed as the very picture of treachery and guile. She exercised profound influence over her husband, Ahab, inciting him to great evil against the prophets of God, as we will see in a future study.

OFFICIAL STATE RELIGION: Ahab takes Jeroboam's idolatry to its logical conclusion. Where Jeroboam mixed true worship with paganism, Ahab embraces pure pagan idolatry.

BAAL: The predominant god in Canaanite religion. The pagans worshiped him as the one who sent rain and provided abundant crops. While Jeroboam had combined paganism with the worship of God, Ahab forsook Israel's God altogether and followed his wife into Baal worship.

32. TEMPLE OF BAAL: Baal, whose name meant "lord, husband, owner," was the predominant god in the Canaanite religion, and by building this temple—with its altar and wooden image—Ahab was promoting Baal worship as the official state religion of Israel. Just as David had captured Jerusalem and his son Solomon had built a temple for the Lord there, so Omri established Samaria and his son Ahab built a temple for Baal there.

33. PROVOKE THE LORD GOD OF ISRAEL TO ANGER: Ahab and Jezebel led the nation of Israel to reject God as their Lord—a sin that Elijah combated during his ministry. In the end, however, Ahab's wickedness paved the way for the final collapse of Israel.

34. HIEL OF BETHEL BUILT JERICHO: The Lord had destroyed Jericho centuries earlier when Joshua led the people of Israel into the Promised Land and had forbidden anyone to rebuild it. However, Joshua had also prophesied that one day a man would do so at the cost of two sons' lives (see Joshua 6:26). This came to pass when two of Hiel's sons died in helping him fortify the city. It is no coincidence that the people of Israel would disregard such a dire warning from the Lord during the days of Ahab's reign, as they were already treating His Word with contempt.

ENTER ELIJAH: In the midst of Israel's wickedness, the Lord shows His mercy by sending a prophet to turn the nation's heart back to Himself.

17:1. ELIJAH THE TISHBITE: The prophet's name means "the LORD is God," and his ministry consisted of urging the people of Israel to recognize God as their Lord. God has sent him to Israel to confront Baalism and to declare that the Lord was God and there was no other. He was from a town named Tishbe, located east of the Jordan near the River Jabbok.

BEFORE WHOM I STAND: Elijah took a firm and public stand for God right from the beginning of his ministry. He then called on the people of Israel to join him and make up their minds whom they would serve. It is a demonstration of God's great mercy to the people of Israel that He would send His prophet to call the people to repentance even in the midst of Ahab's determined wickedness. Elijah was also extremely bold in approaching the king—always without an invitation and generally without a welcome. However, he knew it was as nothing to speak to an earthly king when one stood in the presence of almighty God.

THERE SHALL NOT BE DEW NOR RAIN: The autumn and spring rains and summer dew were necessities for the crops of Israel. The Lord had warned Israel that He would withhold this water from them if they went in pursuit of foreign gods (see Deuteronomy 11:16–17). Yet a drought was also a suitable punishment for a people who ascribed the spring rains to Baal, a false deity who was believed to be god of storms and fertility. Elijah had prayed for the drought, and God had answered. According to James 5:17, it lasted three years and six months.

3. HIDE BY THE BROOK CHERITH: Ahab proved hostile to Elijah's bold pronouncements, so the Lord withdrew His chosen prophet from His people for a season, allowing them to discover what life would be like if they continued to reject Him. The location of the brook is not known, but it was probably a seasonal brook that flowed during the rainy season and dried up when the weather turned hot. It was located east of the Jordan River.

4. I HAVE COMMANDED THE RAVENS: While Ahab was leading Israel to believe that a nonexistent entity called Baal had control over the earth and its forces, the Lord of creation was reminding Elijah that it was *He* who commanded the natural world. "You alone are the LORD, You have made heaven, the heaven of heavens, with all their host, the earth and everything on it" (Nehemiah 9:6).

5. HE WENT AND DID ACCORDING TO THE WORD OF THE LORD: This statement would come to characterize Elijah's life. But his immediate obedience also stood as a condemnation against the kings of Israel, who stubbornly refused to obey God's commands.

MIRACULOUS PROVISION: The Lord provides for Elijah's physical needs, just as He did for Moses and the people of Israel during the exodus from Egypt.

6. THE RAVENS BROUGHT HIM BREAD AND MEAT: The Lord had miraculously provided food and water for the Israelites during their exodus from Egypt. He had rained down manna and poured water from rocks for the Israelites prior to their entry into the Promised Land by crossing the Jordan River. It was a tragic irony here, however, that the prophet of God had been banished to the other side of the Jordan, where he was miraculously provided with food and water while the people of Israel endured a terrible drought.

7. THE BROOK DRIED UP: The Lord is not limited in the methods He uses to accomplish His purposes, and He may choose to "dry up" a source of provision for His people. When He does, however, it is because He intends to provide for His people through another source. Elijah was depending not on the brook but on the God who created the brook. Even though the brook dried up, he knew that his God would continue to provide.

UNLEASHING THE TEXT

1) What was Jehu's prophesy against Baasha? How did that come to pass? What happened after Zimri murdered Baasha's son Elah?

_____

_____

_____

2) What might have motivated Omri's son, Ahab, to become a Baal worshiper? What role might politics have played? What role might Jezebel have played?

_____

_____

_____

3) Why did Ahab view the sins of Jeroboam as though they were trivial things? How did this attitude affect his decisions? How did it affect his influence as king?

_____

_____

_____

4) Why did God send a drought on Israel? Why did He make special provision for Elijah? Why was Elijah given authority to end the drought?

_____

_____

_____

EXPLORING THE MEANING

Sin is never trivial. Jeroboam instituted idolatry in Israel, attempting to mix it with the nation's worship of God. This was a grievous sin for which the Lord judged him, yet Ahab acted "as though it had been a trivial thing" (1 Kings 16:31). By the time Ahab became king, the nation had been embracing Jeroboam's sinful practices for some fifty years, and the people had probably grown so accustomed to it that it seemed normal. This attitude of shrugging off sin led Ahab into even greater wickedness, and eventually it brought about the downfall of all Israel.

Sin is never trivial in God's eyes, but when we as believers in Christ ignore it or indulge in it, we can become inured to it. In fact, we can grow so accustomed to wickedness that we cease to be bothered by it—and even accept it as normal behavior in the world around us. The danger of this nonchalance is that if we don't take sin seriously, we can begin to slide into embracing it ourselves.

God hates sin, and He calls His people to hate it as He does. It is easy to become complacent about disobedience, which is why we must always guard against becoming comfortable with sin by spending time in God's Word and in regular fellowship with other believers. As James warns us, "Friendship with the world is enmity with God. Whoever therefore wants to be a friend of the world makes himself an enemy of God. . . . Draw near to God and He will draw near to you. Cleanse your hands, you sinners; and purify your hearts, you double-minded" (James 4:4, 8).

Do not be unequally yoked. Ahab married a Canaanite woman who worshiped Baal. The Lord had expressly forbidden His people to intermarry with the Canaanites, and He expected His chosen king to lead the people by demonstrating obedience to His commands. Of course, Ahab was not the first king to sin in this way. Solomon took many foreign wives, and the end result was the same for both men: they were led away from the Lord by their unequal marriages.

Jezebel's influence over the king was profound, as we will see in later studies. As a priestess of Baal, she no doubt played an influential role in Ahab's decision to lead the entire nation into Baal worship and paganism. But this is actually no surprise, and in fact it is part of the reason why the Lord commands His people not to marry unbelievers. An unbelieving spouse will *always* exert an ungodly influence on the believer, and all too often that spouse will lead the believer far from obedience to God's Word.

This principle applies today as much as it did in Ahab's time. Paul warns us, "Do not be unequally yoked together with unbelievers. For what fellowship has righteousness with lawlessness? And what communion has light with darkness? And what accord has Christ with Belial? Or what part has a believer with an unbeliever? And what agreement has the temple of God with idols? For you are the temple of the living God" (2 Corinthians 6:14–16).

The Lord provides for His people. God sent a terrible drought against Israel and the surrounding nations as a judgment for the peoples' sin of idolatry, but His servant Elijah never went hungry or thirsty. He did the same for the entire nation of Israel during their exodus from Egypt, providing water in the middle of the desert and food that miraculously rained from above. Even in the midst of God's judgment on Ahab, the Lord would have ended the drought and restored His people if they had only repented of their idolatry.

Of course, God's provision to Elijah does not mean that he did not suffer any hardship. God called him to live in the wilderness and depend on ravens for food and a small brook for water. The Lord even permitted him to face some uncertainty in His miraculous provision when the brook dried up. Yet Elijah's short-term difficulties were far outweighed by God's faithful provision, and the prophet did not go hungry or thirsty.

The Lord has not changed since Elijah's day, and He still provides for His people today. All He asks is for His people to obey His Word and rely on Him for all their needs, and He promises to take care of the rest. Jesus taught us, "Do not worry, saying, 'What shall we eat?' or 'What shall we drink?' or 'What shall we wear?' For after all these things the Gentiles seek. For your heavenly Father knows that you need all these things. But seek first the kingdom of God and His righteousness, and all these things shall be added to you" (Matthew 6:31–33).

Reflecting on the Text

5) What does it mean to view sin as trivial? What sins does the world view as trivial today? Which ones have you sometimes viewed as trivial?

_____

_____

_____

_____

6) What excuses might Ahab have offered for marrying Jezebel? What do you think was God's view of that marriage?

_____

_____

_____

7) What are some of the miraculous provisions that God made for His people in the Bible? What provisions has He made for you at times in your life?

_____

_____

_____

_____

8) If you had been in Elijah's place, how would you have felt about the drought? How would you have felt about the idolatry in Israel? About your situation living next to a brook?

_____

_____

_____

_____

PERSONAL RESPONSE

9) Are there areas of sin in your life that you are choosing to ignore? How do you think the Lord sees those things? What do you need to do to gain God's perspective?

_____

_____

_____

_____

10) What are some of the things that God has provided to you when you
needed them the most? Make a list below, and then take time to thank
the Lord for His love and mercy.

_____

_____

_____

7

Elijah and the Widow
1 Kings 17:8–24

Drawing Near

Why does God often meet our needs on a daily basis rather than a monthly or yearly basis? What would happen to our attitude and mindset if we always had everything we needed?

_____

_____

_____

The Context

The people of Elijah's day were dependent on farming. There were no supermarkets where the people could purchase food, and most of the population lived on what they were able to grow for themselves. If there was no rain, hunger and starvation were real possibilities. Furthermore, because farming was hard work, it was for the most part considered a man's work. A woman and her children depended heavily on the man of the house to provide food and shelter. A widow without family would almost certainly starve to death under normal circumstances—and especially in the midst of the severe drought that took place during Elijah's lifetime.

As it happened, while Elijah was being fed by ravens there was such a widow living in the city of Zarephath. This woman had a young son, and she was very poor. However, what distinguished this woman from her neighbors was not her financial situation but her faith. She lived between Tyre and Sidon, which was the heartland of Baal worship at the time. Indeed, her king was Jezebel's father, a man who hated the people of God as much as his wicked daughter did. Yet here was this woman, in the midst of the pagans, worshiping Israel's God!

One might expect the Lord to bless such a faithful and courageous woman with great wealth and perfect health. But such was not the case. This woman was so poor that she was getting ready to eat her last meal at the moment Elijah arrived, and her son's health was soon to deteriorate and end in sudden death. This woman, it turns out, was actually quite rich, but her wealth was not in gold—it was in a powerful faith and obedience to the King of kings.

The Lord ultimately did honor this poor widow's great faith. But He did so not by showering her with monetary wealth but by giving her yet more faith. The woman's great faith and obedience provide an example for us today.

KEYS TO THE TEXT

Read 1 Kings 17:8–24, noting the key words and phrases indicated below.

> GOD SENDS ELIJAH TO THE HEATHEN: *Elijah has been living by the Brook Cherith for some time, but now the Lord sends him off to the heart of Baal worship.*

8. THEN THE WORD OF THE LORD CAME TO HIM: Elijah had been living by the Brook Cherith for an unspecified amount of time, all the while being fed by ravens. He was depending on the brook for water, yet the Lord allowed it to dry up. There is an old saying that when the Lord closes a door, He opens a window—and this passage provides an excellent example of that principle. The Lord permitted the brook to dry up because He had another job for Elijah in another location. He sometimes calls His servants to trust Him through times of uncertainty or hardship.

9. GO TO ZAREPHATH: This was a town on the Mediterranean coast about midway between Tyre and Sidon (see the map in the Introduction). This territory was ruled by Jezebel's father, Ethbaal, who was also the high priest of Baal at the time. By sending Elijah there, God was revealing His power in the very area where the impotent Baal was worshiped. The location is also significant because it means the widow who would help Elijah was also residing in in the heart of Baal worship. Yet, as we will see, she was faithful to the God of Israel.

I HAVE COMMANDED A WIDOW THERE: This suggests the widow was a follower of God. Like others in Israel, she was obedient to the Lord at the risk of grave danger to herself. After all, if Jezebel did not hesitate to murder the Lord's prophets in Israel, how much more would her father have slaughtered any of God's people in Sidon! The widow's faith in the Lord is even more remarkable given that she was not a Jew and did not live in Israel.

THREE TESTS: The Lord asks the woman to obey Him on faith, even though her actions could prove costly—and could potentially lead to starvation for her and her son.

10. GATHERING STICKS: This underscores the widow's dire poverty. She did not have the materials on hand to even build a fire, let alone enough food to cook a meal.

BRING ME A LITTLE WATER: Elijah's first request might be viewed as a small test to discern whether or not this was the woman to whom God had sent him. The drought was severe, and even a cup of water would have been highly valued, yet this widow left off her task of gathering sticks to go get some for a thirsty stranger. The widow did not know it yet, but she was serving God's anointed prophet—and her reward would be great.

11. BRING ME A MORSEL OF BREAD: Elijah's second request was more severe than it might seem, for he was asking the widow to part with her last meal. In short, Elijah was asking her to put her hope of being provided for completely in the Lord's hands.

12. AS THE LORD YOUR GOD LIVES: The widow here acknowledged that she served the living God. Such words were bold in the gate of a city that was devoted to Baal worship, yet she did not try to hide the fact that she did not serve false gods.

THAT WE MAY EAT IT, AND DIE: The widow was gathering sticks with which to cook the last meal for herself and her son. She had nothing else, and no prospect of getting anything else, and the future (as far as she could discern) held only death by starvation for them both. Her calm demeanor in this situation was striking. She did not engage in any dramatics, nor did she pour out complaints to God's prophet. In fact, she did not even mention her urgent need at Elijah's first request for water, but only when he went on to request food. Her actions and attitude demonstrate that she held a quiet faith in God, and she knew that her future (and her son's future) was in His hands.

13. DO NOT FEAR: Once again we see the importance of courage in the life of faith. Elijah was about to ask the woman to do something that would require great faith, and he knew that fear would prompt the woman to refuse—and if she refused, she would lose an opportunity to see the Lord's miraculous provision for her family. But if she chose to act with courage, obeying the Lord's commands and leaving the consequences to Him, then her obedience would bring great reward and her faith would grow even stronger.

MAKE ME A SMALL CAKE FROM IT FIRST: This request was the most difficult of all for the widow to fulfill. Elijah wanted her to take what little flour she had—barely enough to feed herself and her son—and use a portion of it first to make a cake for him. We can see an increasing difficulty in the three requests of Elijah: (1) "bring me some water," (2) "bring me some food," and then, (3) "make my food first before you feed your starving family." The Lord was emptying this woman of all she could hope in and was leaving her with nothing except her faith. But the Lord already knew that her faith was strong enough before He asked this of her, for He never tests his servants beyond their abilities to pass the test.

15. SHE WENT AWAY AND DID ACCORDING TO THE WORD OF ELIJAH: Remember that this woman was not an Israelite and did not have the rich heritage and teaching of God's Law that was freely available to His people. And yet, in spite of this, she willingly obeyed the prophet's instructions, even at great cost to herself. Meanwhile, the people of Israel willfully disobeyed the prophets and God who had sent them.

16. THE BIN OF FLOUR WAS NOT USED UP: God had miraculously provided manna for His people during their exodus from Egypt, feeding them but not the surrounding nations. Now the tables were turned as the Lord miraculously provided food each morning for this foreign widow while leaving Israel in famine.

DEATH AND RESURRECTION: Some time later the widow's son dies, and she turns to the prophet of God for help. The Lord then strengthens her faith by raising her son back to life.

17. NO BREATH LEFT IN HIM: In other words, the boy died.

18. BRING MY SIN TO REMEMBRANCE: The widow, in her grief, assumed her son had died as some sort of divine retribution for her own sins. This is a common response of human nature in times of great sorrow, but it is not an accurate view of God. The woman was correct in recognizing that her son's life was entirely in God's hands but not in thinking that her son died because of her own sins.

19. THE UPPER ROOM WHERE HE WAS STAYING: Elijah occupied a small room on the rooftop of the house that was accessible only from outside. This afforded him his own private quarters and avoided even the appearance of any inappropriate relationship with the widow.

20. HAVE YOU ALSO BROUGHT TRAGEDY ON THE WIDOW: We can certainly understand why Elijah considered the boy's death a great tragedy. The widow was mystified as to why God would save her boy's life during the famine only to take it now, and Elijah was unable to explain what the Lord was doing.

BY KILLING HER SON: Yet Elijah also recognized that all life is in the hands of God, and that it was God Himself who had allowed this boy to die. His deep grief also indicates how much he cared about the widow and her son.

21. HE STRETCHED HIMSELF OUT ON THE CHILD THREE TIMES: Elijah was not performing mouth-to-mouth resuscitation here, because the boy was not unconscious—he was dead. Why Elijah did this is not clear, but what *is* clear is that Elijah was fervently praying for the boy.

22. THE LORD HEARD THE VOICE OF ELIJAH: The Lord always hears the cries of His children, and He is always faithful to respond. There are times, however, when He waits for us to ask before He sends the answer. Here the Lord showed that the power to raise the boy was found not in Elijah but rather in God, the author of life.

23. YOUR SON LIVES: Canaanite myths claimed that Baal could revive the dead, but here it was the Lord God, not Baal, who was giving back the boy's life. This conclusively demonstrated Yahweh was the only true God and Elijah was His prophet. This is also the first recorded instance of resurrection in the Bible.

24. BY THIS I KNOW THAT YOU ARE A MAN OF GOD: The widow had already placed her faith in God's Word simply by obeying what He asked her to do with her last remnants of food. But here she had seen a dramatic demonstration of God's power that surpassed even the miraculous renewal of food each day, for only God can defeat the powers of death. It is important to recognize, however, that the woman's faith and obedience preceded this great miracle. She obeyed the Lord on faith, and He strengthened that faith with a clear demonstration of His great power and love. The Jews in Jesus' day, by contrast, demanded a sign but were denied it because they had already refused to place their faith and trust in God (see Luke 11:29–32).

UNLEASHING THE TEXT

1) Why did God send Elijah to live with the widow in Zarephath? What did He want to accomplish for the widow? What did he want to accomplish for the people of Zarephath?

_____

_____

_____

_____

2) Why did Elijah ask the woman for water? Why did he ask for food? Why did he insist that she make food for him before making it for herself and her son?

_____

_____

_____

_____

3) Why did the woman honor Elijah's requests, even though he was a complete stranger to her? What did her actions reveal about her faith in God?

_____

_____

_____

4) If you had been in the widow's place, how would you have reacted when your son died? When Elijah asked you for his body? When he was resurrected?

_____

_____

_____

EXPLORING THE MEANING

The Lord sometimes requires obedience before He sends His blessing. The widow in this passage feared God and served Him alone, even though she lived in a land that was openly hostile to the things of God. It was no coincidence that the Lord sent His prophet Elijah to her, because He intended to pour out His blessings on her, providing her with food and water at a time when the rest of the world was starving. But before He demonstrated His power to her, He required that she demonstrate her faith to the world around her.

When we speak of the Lord "testing our faith," we should understand that it is not a test like the ones we were given in school, where the Lord is trying to find out how much faith we have. God already knows our hearts and the strength of our faith. Rather, His tests are designed to demonstrate the extent of our faith—as a testimony to the world that God's children trust Him fully—and to strengthen our faith even further. The widow's faith was strengthened and deepened when she obeyed the Lord's commands, and she also testified to the Baal-centered world around her that the God of Israel was the only true God.

God desires deeply to send blessing on blessing into the lives of His children, but there are times when we cannot fully receive those blessings unless we first obey His Word. The important thing to remember in this regard is that the Lord already knows our limits, and He has promised that He will never send us a test or a trial that is too great for us to bear. As Paul wrote, "No temptation has overtaken you except such as is common to man; but God is faithful, who will not allow you to be tempted beyond what you are able, but with the temptation will also make the way of escape, that you may be able to bear it" (1 Corinthians 10:13).

All life is from God. The death of the young boy in this passage was a terrible blow to the widow, both because of the grief over losing her son and also because, in human terms, he represented her hope for the future. The woman needed her son to grow to manhood and look after her in old age because her husband was already dead. Yet even in her devastating grief, she turned to the Lord for help, by way of His prophet Elijah. She recognized that God was the author of all life and that He alone had authority over death—and resurrection.

There are no recorded instances of someone being brought back from the dead prior to this passage in Scripture. Yet in spite of this fact, the widow was quick to give her dead son into Elijah's hands the moment he asked. Canaanite myths of that time claimed that Baal could restore life to the dead, but needless to say such a thing had never happened. By putting her dead son's body into Elijah's hands, the widow was demonstrating her faith that God had the power all the false gods lacked: the power to restore her son to life.

The Scriptures are emphatic on this point, from the first chapter of Genesis to the final chapter of Revelation: God is the author and sustainer of all life. He spoke life into existence at creation (see Genesis 1), and the river of life flows from His throne in eternity (see Revelation 22). Jesus said, "I am the bread of life" (John 6:48); "I am the resurrection and the life. He who believes in Me, though he may die, he shall live" (John 11:25); and "I am the way, the truth, and the life. No one comes to the Father except through Me" (John 14:6). Life is a gift given directly from the hand of God, and He alone has authority over it.

We are to obey God's Word and leave the consequences in His hands. The Lord asked a starving widow to feed a complete stranger, even as she was gathering twigs to cook her last small bit of flour before facing utter starvation. This was a costly step of faith on her part, as she was responsible not only for her own food but also for feeding her son. As a widow in an agrarian culture, she had no easy way of providing food for her family and no husband who could provide an income. She even faced the prospect of watching her son die with her. Yet the Lord asked her to share what little she had left with a stranger, and she obeyed.

At that point, the widow was demonstrating a deep faith in the character and power of the Lord. She was willing to do what He asked, even though it might potentially mean the end of her family. This is the essence of faith: to obey God's Word simply because He is our Lord, even when there might be some costly consequences as a result of such obedience. Our faith is based on God's faithfulness, and we rest in the assurance that He will work out the future to His glory and our blessing.

The widow was not disappointed . . . and neither will we be when we follow her example. The Lord was not hampered by the drought, and He was fully able to provide her with food and oil for as long as needed. He is not hampered by any circumstances in our lives today either, and He is still faithful to provide for His children's needs. Our job is not to worry about the future but to obey God's Word today, trusting in the fact that He will take care of whatever follows from our obedience.

REFLECTING ON THE TEXT

5) How did the widow's faith contrast with the faith of most Israelites at the time? What spiritual benefits did Israel enjoy that the woman did not have? What blessings did she gain that Israel lacked?

---

6) How strong was the widow's faith in the Lord when she first met Elijah? What did the Lord do to make it even stronger? How had her faith grown by the end of this passage?

_____

_____

_____

_____

7) What was the woman's response to her son's death? Was she wrong for making such an emotional outburst? How do you see her faith even in the way she reacts to this event?

_____

_____

_____

_____

8) When have you obeyed God's Word, even though you were uncertain what consequences it might bring? How did that obedience strengthen your faith?

_____

_____

_____

_____

_____

PERSONAL RESPONSE

9) How well are you trusting the Lord's authority over life and death?
Do you struggle with fears regarding your mortality? Do you trust Him
with the lives of your loved ones?

_____

_____

_____

_____

10) Is the Lord calling you to costly obedience today? If so, what consequences
do you fear? How will you overcome your fear and leave those
consequences in His hands?

_____

_____

_____

_____

8

ELIJAH'S CHALLENGE
1 Kings 18:1–46

DRAWING NEAR

Consider some people in modern times who stood up for their beliefs in spite of the fact that many people opposed them. How does history tend to remember such individuals?

_____

_____

_____

THE CONTEXT

The drought had been going on for several years, and the terrible lack of water had precipitated a famine. Crops had dried up, livestock were dying, and all of Israel was suffering. Ahab was trapped by his own folly. The longer he went worshiping Baal—the supposed god of rain—the more desperate he became and the more the Lord withheld the rain.

However, instead of repenting and turning to God, Ahab and his servant went on a desperate search for enough green grass to feed his remaining livestock. At this same time, the Lord informed Elijah that it was time to end the drought. Elijah obeyed the Lord's command to present himself before Ahab, and along the way he found Ahab's servant searching for grass. Elijah sent word to Ahab of God's intentions, and the king rushed cross-country to meet him.

Yet the problem that brought about the drought in the first place was still present in Israel, as neither Ahab nor the people had repented of their idolatry. So Elijah called for a dramatic confrontation: bring together the prophets of Baal, and let them call on their god to show his power. If Baal had any power, the people would serve him; otherwise, the people would turn back to the true God of Israel.

This is one of the most dramatic passages in the Old Testament, and it demonstrates how God alone controls the world. Elijah was about to have a showdown with the prophets of Baal. And Israel was about to witness a vivid display of the power of their Creator.

KEYS TO THE TEXT

Read 1 Kings 18:1–46, noting the key words and phrases indicated below.

> ENDING THE DROUGHT: *After three and a half years, the Lord tells Elijah that He will bring an end to the drought. Elijah immediately goes to meet Ahab.*

1. I WILL SEND RAIN ON THE EARTH: The Lord had given Elijah the authority to call for the end of the drought (see 1 Kings 17:1), but here we are reminded that only the Lord had control over the natural forces of the earth.

2. ELIJAH WENT TO PRESENT HIMSELF TO AHAB: This was to give Ahab opportunity to repent. He was the cause of the national judgment in the famine, so if he repented, rain would come.

3. OBADIAH: His name means "servant of the LORD." This is not the same man who wrote the Old Testament book of Obadiah. Rather, he was a high-ranking servant of the king "who was in charge of his house," meaning he was Ahab's steward.

A QUIETLY COURAGEOUS MAN: Obadiah is the manager of Ahab's royal palace and holds a very important position in the kingdom. But he is also a servant of the Most High God.

OBADIAH FEARED THE LORD GREATLY: This statement is significant, considering that Obadiah was a trusted servant within the home of Jezebel, a woman who hated God's people to the point that she murdered His prophets. It demonstrates the Lord is capable of placing His servants wherever He chooses—even under the noses of His enemies. It also suggests that Obadiah's faithfulness to the Lord extended to his work and his employers. They trusted him because he was faithful to his duties, which is a mark of one who is obedient to the Lord's commands.

4. JEZEBEL MASSACRED THE PROPHETS OF THE LORD: We are not told how many of God's people were murdered at the hand of Jezebel, but the fact that Obadiah saved 100 suggests that she slaughtered many more than that number. The word translated *massacred* literally means "to cut off or eliminate." Jezebel was attempting to utterly annihilate the people of God who opposed Baal—to cut off and eliminate the Lord's people from the land.

FIFTY TO A CAVE: The area around Carmel included thousands of caves, many of which were large enough to hold fifty men. While the ravens had been feeding Elijah at the brook, Obadiah had been performing the same service for other prophets.

AN UNEXPECTED MEETING: Obadiah encounters Elijah in the wilderness and is pleased—at first. But then he is filled with fear at what he must do next.

6. THEY DIVIDED THE LAND BETWEEN THEM: Here is another powerful testimony of the trust that Ahab placed in Obadiah. The king felt the job of finding grass for his livestock so important that he was willing to walk throughout Israel by himself in search of grass for his livestock. Given this, he would have selected only the most competent and trustworthy man to cover the other half.

7. FELL ON HIS FACE: Obadiah wielded considerable authority as steward of the king's household, yet here he humbled himself to the point of falling on his face before Elijah. He probably also showed respect for the king by virtue of his office as the Lord's chosen ruler over Israel, but he did not put stock in the

trappings of the world. Obadiah was ready to abase himself before those who stood in the presence of the King of kings.

9. How have I sinned: Obadiah's fear was that Ahab would suspect him of some sort of treachery, thinking he was in league with Elijah in some devious plot against his throne. This, of course, was the opposite of the truth, as God's servants were trying to turn the king back to obedience to His commands.

12. the spirit of the Lord will carry you: Obadiah was also afraid that, once he had told Ahab where to find Elijah, the Lord would whisk him away to some distant place. Ahab would then explode in irrational anger and kill his servant. Obadiah viewed himself as being between a rock and a hard place: he was afraid that Elijah would play a trick on him, and he was afraid that Ahab would kill him regardless.

13. Was it not reported to my lord: Obadiah seems to have lost sight of the fact that God saw all his deeds and would not abandon His faithful servant. Obadiah evidently felt the need to remind God of what he had done—fearing that the Lord would not protect him otherwise. His fear caused him to think he had to earn God's favor, when the truth was just the opposite.

In Search of Elijah: When Obadiah returns to Ahab and tells him that Elijah is looking for him, the king breaks with protocol and goes in search of the prophet himself.

16. Ahab went to meet Elijah: A king never went out to meet anyone except another king, but Ahab knew that Elijah was a true prophet of God and that he had the authority to end the drought and famine. So, in his desperation, Ahab threw away kingly convention and rushed out to meet Elijah, even though the prophet was already on his way to meet him.

17. O troubler of Israel: Ahab blamed Elijah for the drought, which was the opposite of the truth. It was God who had sent the drought, not Elijah, and it was Ahab who had moved the Lord's wrath in the first place. Ahab had the fool's habit of accusing others of his own sins.

18. you and your father's house have: Once again, Elijah spoke with amazing temerity. Ahab had accused him of a crime worthy of death, and he had the power to carry out that sentence if he chose. But Elijah knew that even the power of a king was nothing in the presence of God, and he boldly confronted the king with the truth from God.

THE SHOWDOWN: Elijah tells Ahab to assemble the people of Israel on Mount Carmel, where they will see for themselves whether or not Baal can end their drought.

19. GATHER ALL ISRAEL TO ME: Elijah wanted the entire nation to be present for a clear demonstration that the God of Israel was the only One who ruled the earth. His intention was to force the people to decide once and for all whom they would serve: Baal or Yahweh.

MOUNT CARMEL: Carmel was actually a range of mountains, not a single peak. The area was known for its lush tree cover and fruitfulness, so Elijah may have selected the region in order to allow the priests of Baal every advantage in the coming "showdown." The Baal worshipers might have thought their false god was at his greatest strength in such a place, so his defeat would be all the more dramatic.

20. AHAB SENT FOR ALL THE CHILDREN OF ISRAEL: It is interesting that Ahab, the king of Israel, obeyed the command of Elijah. He may have simply been motivated by a desire to end the drought one way or another, yet it is clear he had gained respect for the power of God that was demonstrated in the prophet's life and words.

21. FALTER BETWEEN TWO OPINIONS: The word translated *falter* literally means "to limp," but it is also used in verse 26 to mean "leap about" or "dance." The people of Israel were trying to "dance" back and forth between Baal and Yahweh, but instead they were merely limping along like spiritual cripples. Elijah was determined to force Israel to make a clear-cut choice between Baal and Yahweh, for they were deluding themselves in the belief they could intermingle the two religions into their own syncretistic blend.

THE PEOPLE ANSWERED HIM NOT A WORD: The people's refusal to answer merely underscored their stubborn determination to do things their own way.

22. I ALONE AM LEFT: Elijah was actually not the only prophet who spoke to Israel on the Lord's behalf, but he was alone on that mountaintop. He was emphasizing the fact that the entire nation had wandered away from the Lord, yet he was not daunted by being so outnumbered. Elijah's life was characterized by such courage in speaking God's truth.

24. THE GOD WHO ANSWERS BY FIRE: Baal was supposed to wield control over thunder and lightning and storms, so if he was a true god, this test was well within his power. The Lord, however, is the only One who truly controls the things of this world.

ALL THE PEOPLE ANSWERED: At last the people of Israel had something to say. "Seeing is believing," goes the old saying, and the people evidently thought that such a dramatic test would satisfy their doubts once and for all.

BAAL'S TURN: Elijah allows the false prophets to go first and gives them the entire day to bring down fire from their nonexistent god. They fail.

27. ELIJAH MOCKED THEM: Elijah's mockery actually followed many of the Baal myths, which portrayed the god as musing on actions to take, or fighting a war, or traveling, or even dying and coming back to life. Yet the sarcasm must have hit home for the people of Israel. Despite the popular beliefs of the world around them, the truth was that Baal simply did not exist.

28. CUT THEMSELVES: Pagan worship practices included frenetic dancing and self-mutilation. This self-laceration was practiced to rouse a god's pity and response, but Old Testament law prohibited it (see Leviticus. 19:28; Deuteronomy 14:1).

29. NO ONE PAID ATTENTION: Baal could not pay attention because he didn't exist. In contrast, "The eyes of the LORD run to and fro throughout the whole earth, to show Himself strong on behalf of those whose heart is loyal to Him" (2 Chronicles 16:9).

GOD ACTS: When the false priests are finally exhausted and bloody, Elijah steps up and repairs the altar of God. It's time for the people to see who really controls the heavens and earth.

30. HE REPAIRED THE ALTAR OF THE LORD: This altar had probably been built in earlier days when the people of Israel still worshiped the Lord. It is significant that Elijah refused to touch the altar of Baal but literally rebuilt the worship practices that had been neglected by the people of God.

32 .TWO SEAHS OF SEED: This was about four gallons or one-third of a bushel of seed.

35. HE ALSO FILLED THE TRENCH WITH WATER: Elijah deliberately soaked both wood and sacrifice, even to the point of filling the surrounding trench with water, in order to make it abundantly clear that he was up to no tricks. No human agency would be able to ignite that sacrifice—only fire from heaven would accomplish it.

36. ELIJAH THE PROPHET CAME NEAR AND SAID: Notice the sharp contrast between Elijah's simple prayer and the frenzied self-destruction of the false prophets. We do not need to perform dramatic acts to get God's attention, for He is already attentive to His people. All that is required is for us to speak to Him and listen to His Word. The "evening sacrifice" mentioned in this verse was offered around 3:00 PM (see Exodus 29:38–41; Numbers 28:3–8).

40. SEIZE THE PROPHETS OF BAAL: God's law commanded that false prophets be put to death, as well as those who followed their false teachings (see Deuteronomy 13:1–18). Elijah took advantage of the excited feelings of the people at this point and called on them to seize the priestly imposters and fill the Brook Kishon with their blood. This river, which drained the Jezreel Valley from east to the northwest, was in the valley north of Mount Carmel.

41. THE SOUND OF ABUNDANCE OF RAIN: Elijah had such faith in God's promises that he sent Ahab away before there was even a cloud in the sky. In this way, he effectively instructed Ahab to celebrate the end of the drought before it actually came to pass.

42. HE BOWED DOWN ON THE GROUND: Elijah prayed for rain this time, and God again answered. The prophet's posture in this case indicates both humility and repentance. He was humbling himself before God on behalf of the unfaithful nation of Israel and interceding on their behalf that the Lord would end the drought.

46. ELIJAH . . . RAN AHEAD OF AHAB: It was customary in the ancient Near East for kings to have runners before their chariots, and Elijah showed Ahab his loyalty by rendering to him that service. It's interesting to note that the distance between Carmel and Jezreel was roughly twenty miles—yet the Lord empowered Elijah to outrun the king's chariot! With God's prophet racing like the wind before him, and God's thunderous power roaring at his back, Ahab was once again forced to recognize that Jehovah was the only true God.

UNLEASHING THE TEXT

1) Why did Ahab call Elijah the "troubler of Israel" (1 Kings 18:17)? In what ways did Ahab and his wife, Jezebel, represent the real trouble in the land?

_____

_____

_____

_____

2) Why did Elijah call for this dramatic confrontation with the prophets of Baal? Do you think there could have been another way to confront the nation's idolatry? Explain.

_____

_____

_____

_____

3) Why did Elijah mock the prophets of Baal? What effect might his sarcasm have had on the false prophets? What effect did it have on the people of Israel who were spectators?

_____

_____

_____

_____

4) Why did Elijah have the false prophets slaughtered? What did this reveal about God's attitude toward idolatry? About His attitude toward teachers of false religions?

_____

_____

_____

_____

EXPLORING THE MEANING

Do not fear what men might do. Ahab was the king of Israel, and in that capacity he had the power to execute those whom he deemed his political enemies. In fact, this was a common practice in that day, and many of the kings who preceded Ahab had ruthlessly slaughtered those who posed a threat to their power. Elijah had come before Ahab and publicly condemned the king's wicked idolatry, and had further declared the coming drought and famine would be lifted only when Elijah asked the Lord to do so. If ever Ahab had a public enemy, it was Elijah.

Yet this threat did not daunt Elijah, who continued to confront the king with boldness concerning his great sin of idolatry. Elijah knew that his life was in God's hands, and not even the king of Israel could harm a hair on his head without God's permission. Elijah's focus was entirely on the sovereignty of God, and as a result he did not fear what men might do to him.

This is not an attitude of recklessness, for God's people are not to act irresponsibly, and neither are we to wantonly disobey those whom God has placed in authority over us. But Elijah had been sent to Ahab with a message from God, and he knew that his job was to obey God's command— regardless of what Ahab might do in retaliation. His priority was to do as he was told and leave the rest in God's hands. As the psalmist put it, "The LORD is on my side; I will not fear. What can man do to me?" (Psalm 118:6).

Be bold to speak God's truth, even when you are the only one. Imagine how Elijah must have felt when he stood on Mount Carmel all by himself, facing 850 hostile pagan priests, a powerful king who was looking for an excuse to execute him, and a crowd of Israelites who were indifferent at best to his fate. The entire nation had at least adulterated their worship practices with paganism, and the most powerful and influential in the land had embraced Baal outright. What's more, the priests of Baal had official endorsement from the queen herself. They were the appointed leaders of the official state religion, and arguing against them was just not done.

Yet Elijah stood on the mountainside and did just this—he argued loudly and urgently against the false teachings of the world around him, even though nobody came up and stood beside him. Christians may find themselves in similar situations, especially as the world continues to move more openly into all manner of heathenism. It can be intimidating to take a stand against the false doctrines of the world today, but God calls us to do so nonetheless.

It is important to remember two points in this regard. First, Elijah may have felt alone, but in fact the Lord had preserved a remnant in Israel of those who were faithful to Him. Second, Elijah would not have been alone even if he *had* been the last faithful man in Israel—for he stood in the presence of the Almighty. The anger of those around him was ultimately not directed at him but at God, and God would never abandon His devoted prophet. When we remember that we serve an omnipotent God who is always holding us in His hand, we will be encouraged to stand up boldly—even if we stand alone.

No one can serve two masters. The people of Israel wanted to have multiple gods. Many didn't want to completely abandon the God of Israel—perhaps because they enjoyed the traditions and practices associated with worshiping Him—but at the same time they also wanted to worship Baal. The endorsement of the king and queen had led to Baal worship becoming expected of everyone in Israel, at least to some extent, so the Israelites didn't see a problem with mixing the two together. The result was a self-designed religion that was guaranteed to fit everyone's individual needs and desires.

The problem was that there is, in eternal reality, only one God, and He has described Himself as "a jealous God" (Exodus 34:14). He would not share the peoples' worship with anything or anybody else. As we have seen, it is possible to make idols out of almost anything in this world, and when we allow something to become an idol, we effectively make it master of our life. Whatever we idolize will demand our time, attention, and energy, and this demand gives it mastery over us.

Money provides an excellent example of this pattern. We make money a priority when we begin to worry about tomorrow's expenses or begin to focus our attention on how to get more. Money quickly becomes a driving force in our lives, an idol, and therefore our master. Jesus warned about this trap: "No one can serve two masters; for either he will hate the one and love the other, or else he will be loyal to the one and despise the other. You cannot serve God and mammon [money]" (Matthew 6:24).

REFLECTING ON THE TEXT

5) Why did the people of Israel "falter between two opinions" (1 Kings 18:21)? How did they get to that point? What was required to end their vacillation?

_____

_____

_____

_____

6) How was Elijah able to be so bold in his dealings with Ahab? Why did he not fear Ahab's wrath? How might his ministry have been different if he had been fearful?

_____

_____

_____

_____

7) How did God demonstrate His wrath in this story? What elements of His grace and mercy did he demonstrate? How does His character display both His justice and mercy in perfect balance?

_____

_____

_____

_____

8) What is so dangerous about intermingling Christianity with the teachings and practices of the world? How does this happen? How does it lead Christians away from God?

_____

_____

_____

_____

Personal Response

9) Is there anything in your life that threatens to become an idol (something that vies against the Lord for mastery)? If so, what will you do this week to remove those threats?

_____

_____

_____

10) When have you taken a bold stand for the Lord, even though you felt alone? What resulted from that stand? Is the Lord calling you to take such a stand at present?

_____

_____

_____

_____

9

ELIJAH'S ESCAPE
1 Kings 19:1–21

DRAWING NEAR

Why are disappointment and discouragement such powerful weapons in Satan's arsenal?

_____

_____

_____

THE CONTEXT

The Lord had demonstrated His power and authority in a dramatic way on Mount Carmel. Elijah had proven to the nation of Israel that Baal did not exist and that Yahweh was the one true God worthy of their worship. The false prophets of Baal had been put to death, just as God's Word commanded, and the people of Israel had been brought to the point of choosing to serve God once and for all. Elijah's ministry had triumphed, and a day of revival was sure to follow.

Or at least that is what Elijah evidently thought. However, the people of Israel were so committed to paganism by this point that not even the miraculous event of God sending fire from heaven to consume water-soaked logs could turn the tide. Jezebel was still queen, and she was still not willing to bend her knee to the God of Israel. Moreover, Elijah was about to discover that she was not happy about the loss of her 850 favorite priests. Jezebel had hardened her heart against the Lord, and not even a miracle was going to soften it.

In her anger, Jezebel sent a message to Elijah that she was going to have him put to death just as he had ordered the death of her false prophets. Elijah had just witnessed the awesome power of God and won a decisive victory over Baal, but when he heard the message, he immediately arose and fled in fear for his life. He viewed Jezebel's opposition as a personal attack, and he could not understand how she could still reject the Lord.

Elijah became so deeply discouraged as he hid out in the wilderness that he actually prayed for God to take his life. But the Lord still had plans for Elijah, and he still had work for his prophet to do. So, in response, the Lord would intervene in Elijah's life and give him a word of encouragement that he would never forget.

KEYS TO THE TEXT

Read 1 Kings 19:1–21, noting the key words and phrases indicated below.

THE WRATH OF JEZEBEL: Ahab returns home and reports to his wife all that happened on Mount Carmel. Jezebel responds by vowing to put Elijah to death.

1. AHAB TOLD JEZEBEL ALL THAT ELIJAH HAD DONE: There is almost a sense here of subservience, as Ahab reports to his wife. There is no question that she took the leadership in their household (as we will see in our next study), and probably also in many political affairs.

2. MAKE YOUR LIFE AS THE LIFE OF ONE OF THEM: It is interesting that Ahab took no apparent interest in the fate of the 850 false prophets, but Jezebel certainly did. It was through her efforts that further persecution broke out against Elijah and other prophets of God. This suggests once again the amount of influence she had over the king's idolatrous practices. Even after the dramatic demonstration of God's power at Mount Carmel, she still refused to repent of her idolatry. Like Pharaoh in Egypt, she had completely hardened her heart against the Lord, and no display of His presence and power would move her to humble herself before Him.

3. RAN FOR HIS LIFE: It is hard to understand why the bold prophet who confronted kings, called down fire from heaven, and slaughtered false prophets would

suddenly turn and flee from Jezebel. It is true that she was far more likely to carry out her threats against his life than Ahab, but we have already seen how Elijah placed his trust firmly in God's sovereign hand. It appears that Elijah expected Jezebel to surrender, and when she did not capitulate, he became a discouraged man. James reminds us that "Elijah was a man with a nature like ours" (James 5:17), and he was certainly subject to the same human weaknesses as everyone else.

WENT TO BEERSHEBA: This city was located 100 miles south of Jezreel in the Negev. It marked the southern boundary of the population of Judah.

4. BROOM TREE: A desert bush that grew to approximately ten feet in height. It had slender branches with small leaves and fragrant blossoms.

IT IS ENOUGH: Elijah had spent the past three and a half years in hiding, and now his nation had rejected him in spite of the fact that the Lord had used him to end the drought. Elijah was focusing on how people responded to his ministry rather than on how the Lord had used him. This is a surefire recipe for discouragement, and even the great prophet was no exception.

TAKE MY LIFE: Even in his despair, Elijah recognized that his life was in God's hands—though he had temporarily forgotten this truth in the face of Jezebel's threats. Yet he no longer wanted to continue in his lonely ministry, and because the Israelites believed suicide was an affront to the Lord, the prophet asked God Himself to take his life. Job, Moses, Jeremiah, and Jonah also reacted in similar fashion during their ministries (see Job 6:8–9; Numbers 11:10–15; Jeremiah 20:14–18; and Jonah 4:3, 8).

I AM NO BETTER THAN MY FATHERS: Israel's spiritual leaders had all faced rejection from their own people. Samuel was rejected in favor of a king (see 1 Samuel 8:7), and even Moses felt distressed because of Israel's stubbornness (see Numbers 11:1–5). Elijah was no different.

GOD PROVIDES FOR HIS SERVANT: *Elijah is overcome with misery and exhaustion, but an angel of God appears to provide him sustenance.*

5. AN ANGEL TOUCHED HIM: Often in the Bible, we find the Lord sending an angel to minister to his people during times of difficulty. This happened even to Jesus Himself (Matthew 4:11).

6. CAKE BAKED ON COALS, AND A JAR OF WATER: The Lord met Elijah's needs as He did at Cherith, but this time the hand of an angel delivered the food

rather than the beaks of ravens. The Lord was keeping Elijah alive in order to bring him to Mount Horeb.

7. THE JOURNEY IS TOO GREAT FOR YOU: The Lord knows the limitations of His servants better than they do. Elijah thought he had reached the end of his strength, but the Lord still had more for him to accomplish. For those times when the work did actually exceed Elijah's capabilities, the Lord provided miraculous sustenance that enabled him to accomplish it.

8. FORTY DAYS AND FORTY NIGHTS: Elijah's trip took more than double the time it should have taken, which indicates the period had symbolic meaning as well as the literal time it took for the prophet to reach the destination. Just as the people of Israel experienced a notable spiritual failure and so wandered forty years in the wilderness (see Numbers 14:26–35), so a discouraged Elijah would spend forty days in the desert. In addition, just as Moses had spent forty days and nights on Mount Sinai without bread and water (see Exodus 24:18), and Jesus would spend forty days and nights in the wilderness (see Matthew 4:2), so Elijah would spend forty days depending on God's enablement as he prepared for a new commission.

HOREB, THE MOUNTAIN OF GOD: This is an alternate name for Mount Sinai, located approximately 200 miles south of Beersheba. The Lord was bringing Elijah to the very place where Moses had been charged with giving the Law to the Jews. This place not only represented the Law but also the fact that God had chosen a leader to bring His people into the land. Now that the people had rejected Elijah, he came to this place to seek the Lord.

THE STILL SMALL VOICE: The Lord appears to Elijah on Mount Horeb not in the fury of a windstorm, earthquake, or fire, but in the form of a gentle whisper.

9. WHAT ARE YOU DOING HERE: Evidently Elijah had gone to Mount Horeb on his own initiative rather than at the Lord's command. Given that God had appeared to Moses on this mountain, it is possible Elijah wanted to meet with God in the same manner.

10. I HAVE BEEN VERY ZEALOUS: Elijah was not in a fit of self-pity as much as he was simply shocked at how unbelieving Israel had become. The situation was so bad that he had gone back to Egypt, as if he wanted the Lord

to forget about Israel and start over with a new people in a new place. He viewed the Israelites as rebels against the Mosaic covenant—a rebellion that he had been unable to arrest.

THE CHILDREN OF ISRAEL HAVE FORSAKEN YOUR COVENANT: Moses had faced a similar situation when he came down from Mount Sinai and found the people worshiping a golden calf. On that occasion, Moses responded with intercession before the Lord on behalf of Israel (see Exodus 32:11–13). Moses remembered that the Lord is in control of all things and that He loved the people of Israel deeply. Likewise, Elijah had interceded for his people back at Mount Carmel and was now despairing over their unbelief. He saw no hope for Israel's future.

I ALONE AM LEFT: Strictly speaking, as the Lord would shortly reveal, there were other Israelites who had not worshiped Baal. Yet Elijah did not know any of them, so he appealed to God for help. The Lord assured him that his statement was not true.

11. GO OUT, AND STAND ON THE MOUNTAIN BEFORE THE LORD: In the Old Testament, the Lord often revealed his presence through destructive forces such as wind, earthquakes, and fire. These forces indicate His power or His wrath, but they do not summarize His character. God is powerful and just, yet He is also gentle and merciful. Elijah's ministry had been focused on God's justice and His wrath against Israel's unfaithfulness, but the prophet was now going to learn about God's love and mercy.

12. A STILL SMALL VOICE: God does work in dramatic ways, and He often reveals His terrifying power and fury. But He also works in gentle ways, and in this instance He wanted Elijah to see the time for judgment had not yet come. The lesson for Elijah was that the Almighty God was quietly at work in the lives of many people within Israel, even during those dark days under Ahab and Jezebel's rule.

A MISSION RENEWED: The Lord now gives his prophet Elijah a new mission and reassures him that not everyone in Israel has bowed down to the pagan god Baal.

13. WHAT ARE YOU DOING HERE: The Lord repeated His previous question, and Elijah repeated his previous answer verbatim.

15. THE WILDERNESS OF DAMASCUS: God instructed Elijah to go to the Syrian Desert, located south and east of the city of Damascus, and anoint

Hazael of Syria (see 2 Kings 8:8), Jehu (see 2 Kings 9:2), and Elisha (see 1 Kings 19:19) for the purpose of commissioning them to destroy Baal worship in Israel. These three men would complete the work that Elijah began, effectively rooting out Baal worship from Israel. Elijah had tried to abandon Israel, but now God was sending him back with a task: to hand off his ministry to others.

16. ELISHA THE SON OF SHAPHAT: In fact, Elijah would only directly commission Elisha (whose name means "my God is salvation") for this task. Elisha would be involved in Hazael becoming Syria's king (see 2 Kings 8:7–14), and one of Elisha's associates would anoint Jehu (see 2 Kings 9:1–3). By the time the last of these men died, Baalism had been officially barred from Israel.

ABEL MEHOLAH: This hometown of Elisha was located in the Jordan Valley, ten miles south of Beth-Shanon, in the tribal allotment of Manasseh.

18. ALL WHOSE KNEES HAVE NOT BOWED TO BAAL: The Lord assured Elijah that He was still powerfully at work in the lives of His people, preserving 7,000 who had not been seduced by idolatry. Such power is often not dramatic, which is what the Lord was showing Elijah in the still small voice, but it is no less the powerful work of God.

ELIJAH'S SUCCESSOR: Elijah follows God's command and arrives in the town of Abel Meholah, where he meets one the men whom God has said will complete his work.

19. WHO WAS PLOWING WITH TWELVE YOKE OF OXEN: When Elijah found Elisha, he was plowing a field with twelve yoke of oxen. It was a common practice of the time for several teams of oxen, each with his own plow and driver, to work together in a row. Elijah allowed the other drivers to pass and then threw his mantle around the last man, Elisha, to designate him as his successor.

20. GO BACK AGAIN: Elijah told Elisha to go back home and say goodbye to his mother and father, but to keep in mind the solemn call of God and not to allow any earthly affection to detain his obedience.

21. TOOK A YOKE OF OXEN AND SLAUGHTERED THEM: Elisha's slaughter of the oxen was a farewell feast for his family and indicated that he was making a decisive break from them to follow Elijah. He would become Elijah's servant or, literally, his "aide," the same term used for Joshua's relationship

with Moses (see Exodus 24:13; 33:11). Just as Elijah resembled Moses, so Elisha resembled Joshua.

UNLEASHING THE TEXT

1) If you had been in Elijah's place, how might you have expected Jezebel to react to the events on Mount Carmel? If you had been in her place, how might you have responded?

_____

_____

_____

_____

_____

2) Why did Elijah flee to the wilderness? What did he hope to find there? What did he actually find?

_____

_____

_____

_____

_____

3) What caused Elijah to despair? Why did he run away in spite of the fact that he had just witnessed God perform a powerful miracle on Mount Carmel?

_____

_____

_____

4) Why did God prevent Elijah from leaving Israel permanently? What might God have been trying to help Elijah see?

_____

_____

_____

EXPLORING THE MEANING

God is sovereign even when His message is rejected. What a dramatic contrast we see in this episode between Elijah's bold courage on Mount Carmel and his discouraged hopelessness on Mount Horeb. It is easy to understand why he was so distraught. The fire God sent from heaven, the great victory over the priests of Baal, the dramatic run from Carmel to Jezreel, and the joyful end to the drought *should* have caused the Israelites to repent and serve the Lord.

However, instead of repenting, Jezebel said that she wanted Elijah dead, and the Israelites did not defend him. Elijah's words to God reveal the deeper source of his despair: he thought he was the only true follower of Yahweh left, and he was jealous for God's glory. Elijah had his focus on Jezebel's rejection of God and the people's failure to overthrow the false religion of Baal, and he could not reconcile that rejection with the idea of a sovereign God.

Yet God is still in control, even when His message is rejected. Elijah needed to remember that Moses was likewise rejected by the people, but the Lord still brought them into Israel—albeit forty years later. Elijah was not allowed to walk away because the Lord was not done with him yet. In the same way, God calls believers in Christ to be faithful evangelists—yet at the same time, to realize that they are powerless to save anyone. While the world may reject the message, God still remains in control.

We live in the age of grace—but the day of God's wrath is coming. Elijah's ministry was characterized by great drama. He prayed, and the Lord closed the heavens, sending a terrible drought and famine that lasted more than three years. He prayed again, and the Lord opened the heavens. He prayed another time, and the Lord sent down fire that consumed everything in its path. Yet God also wanted Elijah to learn about His less visible ways of working in the world.

The Lord's message to Elijah on Mount Horeb was that He was powerfully at work in Israel even when the fire and fury were not raining down. In the same way, He is constantly at work in the hearts and lives of people today through His Holy Spirit and His Word, and He has provided incalculable grace through the death and resurrection of His Son Jesus. We live in this age of grace and receive eternal life and forgiveness of sin simply through faith in Jesus Christ.

But we must also not lose sight of the fact that the day of grace will come to an end—and after that will come God's terrible judgment. Elijah was not wrong when he anticipated that God would move through the fire and earthquake; it was just not the complete picture. God is merciful and gracious, but He is also just, and in the day of His justice there will be dreadful fire and sorrow. As Paul warned, "We then, as workers together with Him also plead with you not to receive the grace of God in vain. For He says: 'In an acceptable time I have heard you, and in the day of salvation I have helped you.' Behold, now is the accepted time; behold, now is the day of salvation" (2 Corinthians 6:1–2).

The Lord takes care of His own. During the terrible drought and famine in Israel, the Lord provided Elijah with food and water. When the prophet was completely exhausted, God provided more sustenance. Moses received the same provisions during the forty days and nights that he spent on Mount Sinai, and the Father sustained Jesus during His forty days in the wilderness.

The people of Israel enjoyed manna and quail during their sojourn in the desert, and the Lord miraculously supplied water from rocks when they needed it.

The Lord's provision was not just restricted to Elijah's physical needs. He knew that His prophet needed to refocus his attention on the character of God and get his eyes off himself, so He gave him a personal demonstration of His gentleness and grace—which was just what His servant needed at the time. He knew that the work in Israel was too large for Elijah, so He brought along others to carry on for him. He did the same for Moses when His servant was overcome with discouragement (see Numbers 11:15–17).

The Lord understands the human frame better than anyone. After all, He created it from dust, and He also took on human form Himself and experienced firsthand what it means to be human. He provides for His servants' needs because He understands those needs—better than we do ourselves—and because He loves each of His children deeply. Jesus understood our need for God's help, and He sent us the ultimate Helper in the person of the Holy Spirit. "I will pray the Father," He said before His ascension, "and He will give you another Helper, that He may abide with you forever—the Spirit of truth, whom the world cannot receive, because it neither sees Him nor knows Him; but you know Him, for He dwells with you and will be in you. I will not leave you orphans; I will come to you" (John 14:16–18).

REFLECTING ON THE TEXT

5) What do the wind, earthquake, and fire reveal about God's character? Why was He not in them during His encounter with Elijah?

---

6) What does the still small voice reveal about God's character? Why did He choose that means to communicate with Elijah? What was He teaching His servant?

_____

_____

_____

_____

7) How did discouragement influence Elijah's actions and attitudes in this chapter? When have you experienced similar discouragement or despair? How has it affected your actions and attitudes?

_____

_____

_____

_____

8) How can you maintain your trust in God's sovereignty even when people are rejecting His message? What is your responsibility when it comes to sharing the message of Christ?

_____

_____

_____

_____

PERSONAL RESPONSE

9) Do you know someone who is struggling with discouragement? If so, how can you act as a "ministering angel" to help that person?

_____

_____

_____

_____

10) How has the Lord provided for you in the past week? Make a list below of His recent provisions, and then spend time in prayer and thanksgiving.

_____

_____

_____

_____

10

A WICKED PARTNERSHIP
1 Kings 21:1–29

DRAWING NEAR

What are some of the benefits that come from two people working closely in partnership with one another? What are some of the potential pitfalls of such a relationship?

_____

_____

_____

THE CONTEXT

Sometime after Elijah's encounter with God on Mount Horeb, the king of Syria gathered a huge army and attacked Israel (see 1 Kings 20). The Syrians were a world superpower, and their army vastly outnumbered that of the Israelites. But the Lord sent word to Ahab that He intended to give Israel a great victory over Syria. He would do this for the express purpose of once again showing the Israelites that He was their God and that He alone could save them.

As promised, the Lord enabled the Israelites to triumph over the army of Syria in a short battle fought in the hills and valleys surrounding Samaria. The king of Syria, however, did not learn his lesson, and he determined that Israel's God had won the victory because He was God of the hills. Therefore, he led his army against Israel once again, but this time he determined to fight on the open plains, where Israel's God would have no authority. So the Lord sent a prophet to Ahab once again, telling him that He would utterly defeat Syria once and for all. In this way, the Lord would demonstrate to all the world that He was God over all creation.

The Lord kept His word, delivering the Syrian army into Israel's hands. Unfortunately, Ahab then made the choice to disobey the Lord yet again. Ahab's job was to put the king of Syria to death, but instead he made a treaty and sent the king back to his country in peace. So the Lord sent a prophet one more time—but this time the messenger informed Ahab that God would demand his life in exchange for the king of Syria.

Ahab's next move was to conspire with his wife to murder a man named Naboth so he could steal his vineyard. In response, the Lord sent Elijah to deliver a message to the king: "In the place where dogs licked the blood of Naboth, dogs shall lick your blood, even yours" (1 Kings 21:19). Ahab and Jezebel had committed grievous acts of wickedness, and the time was quickly approaching when the Lord would judge them for their deeds.

KEYS TO THE TEXT

Read 1 Kings 21:1–29, noting the key words and phrases indicated below.

COVETING A VINEYARD: *King Ahab looks out his window and sees his neighbor's vineyard—and decides that he must have it. But the neighbor won't sell.*

1. AFTER THESE THINGS: The Syrian king who had attacked Israel was likely Ben-Hadad II, the son or grandson of Ben-Hadad I, who ruled c. 860–841 BC. The Lord had commanded Ahab to execute this king after the battle, but Ahab had allowed himself to be bribed and gave Ben-Hadad II his freedom. The Lord then sent a prophet to Ahab, telling him that his life would be forfeited for his failure to obey God's commands. "After these things" Ahab returned to his palace in Jezreel, where he lived when not residing in his capital at Samaria.

2. GIVE ME YOUR VINEYARD: The Canaanite nations around Israel commonly bought and sold land, much as we do today. The Israelites, however, out of obedience to God's commands did not sell their land. One would expect the king of Israel to understand this, but Ahab had been so influenced by his wife's Canaanite ways that he had adopted them for himself. Evidently, he expected the people of Israel to adopt them as well. Rather than leading God's people in obedience to the Lord's commands, Ahab was leading Israel into the ways of the pagans.

3. THE LORD FORBID: The Lord had commanded the Israelites to not buy and sell their property in Canaan because the land belonged to Him and He wanted His people to be "strangers and sojourners" there (Leviticus 25:23–28). Each tribe and family had received an allotment of land as an "inheritance," and this land was to be viewed as a permanent heritage not to be sold or bartered away. Naboth stood in stark contrast to the king when he refused to disobey the Lord's commands, and his obedience shamed Ahab.

A ROYAL TEMPER TANTRUM: Ahab responds to not getting his way by stomping into his bedroom, lying down on his bed, and refusing to eat.

4. SULLEN AND DISPLEASED: Ahab was pouting because Naboth's obedience to the Lord's directives had highlighted his own disobedience. Notice how childish Ahab's behavior is—he lies on his bed, pouts, and refuses to eat, like a spoiled brat. This is the same king who had recently led the nation of Israel into a miraculous rout against a more powerful enemy! Ahab's behavior underscores the fact that Israel's victory over Syria had been entirely the Lord's doing, and it also shows the true nature of stubborn disobedience. Those who refuse to obey the Word of God are like Ahab— stubborn children who pout when they can't have their own way.

5. JEZEBEL HIS WIFE: The author of Kings frequently refers to Jezebel as Ahab's wife, which reminds us of Ahab's sin in marrying such a heathen in the first place.

6. I SPOKE TO NABOTH THE JEZREELITE: One can almost hear the whine in Ahab's voice.

7. YOU NOW EXERCISE AUTHORITY OVER ISRAEL: Jezebel's statement can be taken as an exclamation or a question. Either way, she was rebuking

Ahab for not exercising absolute royal power in the matter. It is a sad commentary that Ahab, the king of God's chosen people, had to be rebuked in this way for his childlike behavior by a committed pagan who hated the Lord and had murdered hundreds of His prophets.

I WILL GIVE YOU THE VINEYARD: Once again, Jezebel takes the helm of leadership both in Ahab's household and over the nation of Israel.

JEZEBEL TAKES CHARGE: The queen steps in on her husband's behalf and hatches a wicked plot to cheat Naboth out of his land— and his life.

8. SHE WROTE LETTERS IN AHAB'S NAME: This clearly demonstrates the degree of Jezebel's power in Israel. In ancient times, royal scribes wrote letters on a scroll sealed in clay or wax with the sender's personal signature. The seal made the contents of the letters a royal mandate and implied that disobedience would lead to some kind of punishment. When a king permitted another person to use his seal, it indicated an absolute trust in that individual, for the person so entrusted was acting in the place of the king.

9. PROCLAIM A FAST: Calling on the people to humble themselves and fast implied that the Lord was sending a judgment on them. The people would have assumed there was some grievous sin in their midst and would have been quick to put to death whoever the culprit was (see Joshua 7). This is a terrific irony, for there actually *was* grievous sin in Israel—the sin of Baal worship—but it was not faithful men like Naboth who were responsible.

10. SEAT TWO MEN, SCOUNDRELS, BEFORE HIM: Jezebel sent letters to the elders and nobles of Jezreel and told them to find two scoundrels (literally "sons of Belial") to falsely accuse Naboth of committing blasphemy against God and the king of Israel. Under Mosaic Law the penalty for this crime was death, and two witnesses were required for the charge to stand. "Whoever kills a person, the murderer shall be put to death on the testimony of witnesses; but one witness is not sufficient testimony against a person for the death penalty" (Numbers 35:30).

13. THEY TOOK HIM OUTSIDE THE CITY AND STONED HIM WITH STONES: Here is yet another bitter irony: the people of Israel refused to obey the Lord's commands concerning idolatry, yet they carefully followed the law in stoning an innocent man by taking him outside the city gates (see Leviticus 24:14;

Numbers 15:35–36). Naboth was put to death in the open fields along with his sons (2 Kings 9:26), which effectively removed all his heirs.

14. THEN THEY SENT TO JEZEBEL: The fact the elders contacted Jezebel rather than the king might suggest they knew the plot was from her hand, even though the orders had been sealed by the king's signet. This and the fact they murdered Naboth's sons suggest that the elders of the city were complicit in this wicked crime.

THE LORD'S JUDGMENT FALLS: The Lord sends Elijah to inform Ahab that God's wrath is about to fall on his household. The Lord had warned of such judgment in His Law.

18. THERE HE IS, IN THE VINEYARD OF NABOTH: Ahab and Jezebel thought they could hide their wicked deeds, but the Lord saw everything they did. God was watching Ahab enter Naboth's vineyard even as He was sending Elijah to meet him.

19. DOGS SHALL LICK YOUR BLOOD: Elijah's first announcement of judgment applied to Ahab personally. He said the dogs would lick Ahab's blood in the same place where Naboth died, outside the city of Jezreel. Ahab repented when he heard Elijah's dire warning, so the Lord did not carry out this prophecy—at least not entirely. Dogs did end up licking Ahab's blood, but it happened by the pool in Samaria (see 1 Kings 22:37–38).

20. O MY ENEMY: This is the mindset of a man who has hardened his heart to the Lord. Elijah was not Ahab's enemy. In fact, the prophet was actually trying to turn the king away from his path of self-destruction—and he was trying to turn the entire nation of Israel away from it as well. But Ahab could only see that Elijah was opposing his stubborn self-will.

YOU HAVE SOLD YOURSELF: Ahab didn't realize that he had, in fact, sold his soul in exchange for short-term gains. Jesus would later state, "What profit is it to a man if he gains the whole world, and loses his own soul? Or what will a man give in exchange for his soul? For the Son of Man will come in the glory of His Father with His angels, and then He will reward each according to his works" (Matthew 16:26).

21. I WILL TAKE AWAY YOUR POSTERITY: Elijah's second announcement of judgment applied to Ahab and his house. This judgment was virtually

identical with the one made to Jeroboam (see 1 Kings 14:10–11) and was similar to the one made to Baasha (see 16:3–4).

22. LIKE THE HOUSE OF JEROBOAM: The Lord had repeatedly warned His people that if they chased after false gods, He would send calamity on them. This calamity would end, the Lord warned, in Israel being taken into captivity. "Just as the LORD rejoiced over you to do you good and multiply you, so the LORD will rejoice over you to destroy you and bring you to nothing; and you shall be plucked from off the land which you go to possess. Then the LORD will scatter you among all peoples, from one end of the earth to the other, and there you shall serve other gods, which neither you nor your fathers have known—wood and stone" (Deuteronomy 28:63–64). This prophecy would ultimately come to pass.

23. CONCERNING JEZEBEL: Jezebel was the only queen singled out for judgment in the long list of wicked kings in Israel. She had taken authority on herself, both in her home and in the nation, so the Lord held her to the same level of accountability as He did the king. Elijah's prophecy concerning her would be literally fulfilled when the wild dogs outside Jezreel ate her flesh, leaving only her skull, feet, and palms of her hands (see 2 Kings 9:30–37).

24. THE DOGS SHALL EAT: The ultimate disgrace was to die and remain unburied, so that birds and wild animals devoured one's remains. Yet the Lord had warned of this consequence when His people chased after false gods (see Deuteronomy 28:26).

25. BECAUSE JEZEBEL HIS WIFE STIRRED HIM UP: Ahab was capable of being strong and courageous, such as when he led his army into battle, but at home he was weak and contemptible. He permitted his wife to take the headship—and her headship ultimately reached beyond their home to include Ahab's kingly authority. He might have been a very different king if he had not disobeyed the Lord's injunction against marrying foreign wives.

27. HE TORE HIS CLOTHES: The tearing of garments was a common expression of grief, terror, or repentance in the face of great personal or national calamity. Ahab's repentance was genuine, though not complete (see 1 Kings 22). Unfortunately, it came too late, for the Lord's judgment had already fallen on him. Ahab's repentance may have bought him some time, but it did not remove the consequences of his sin.

29. IN THE DAYS OF HIS SON: Because Ahab had truly humbled himself before the Lord, he did not see the disaster that had been forecast for his house. Instead,

God postponed it until the reign of his son, Joram (c. 852–841 BC). Joram would die in Naboth's field (see 2 Kings 9:24–26), bringing an end to Ahab's line.

UNLEASHING THE TEXT

1) Why did Ahab want Naboth's vineyard? What would he have gained by owning it? What does this reveal about Ahab's character?

_____

_____

_____

2) Why did Naboth refuse to sell his land? What might he have gained by selling it? What did he lose by refusing? What does this reveal about Naboth's priorities?

_____

_____

_____

_____

3) How did Jezebel's solution to the vineyard problem compare with Ahab's solution? How might her idolatry have influenced her approach to the problem?

_____

_____

_____

4) What was the result of Naboth's faithfulness to God's commands? What does this teach us about the Christian life? What does it teach us about the possibility that we will face suffering when we choose to follow Christ?

EXPLORING THE MEANING

Coveting is a form of idolatry. Ahab looked out from his mighty palace and noticed an insignificant piece of property nearby. It was a neighbor's vineyard—nothing fancy or large, just a nice little piece of land that would be suitable for a vegetable garden. Perhaps Ahab had developed a sudden urge to take up gardening, or perhaps he had just developed a sudden craving for the land simply because he didn't own it. Whatever his reasons, he began to covet that land above all other things.

It seems odd at first glance that the king of Israel, who had immense wealth and power, would work himself into such a state over a vegetable garden. However, we must remember that Ahab was an idolater. He had forsaken the one true God of heaven and earth in favor of a piece of wood made by men—he had forsaken the Creator in favor of the creation—and it was only natural that he should continue to set his heart on the things of this earth.

The Bible is clear that covetousness is the same as idolatry. We begin to covet when we set our hearts and minds on the material and temporal things of this world rather than on the eternal things of God. When we place things at a higher priority than the Lord, it becomes a form of idolatry, and the only solution to this problem is to refocus our minds on the Lord and His Word. As the apostle Paul warned, "For this you know, that no fornicator, unclean person, nor covetous man, *who is an idolater*, has any inheritance in the kingdom of Christ and God" (Ephesians 5:5, emphasis added).

Obedience to God's Word sometimes leads to suffering—but it is still the best plan. As the king of Israel, Ahab of all people should have understood that the people of Israel were not permitted to sell their land. The land belonged to God; He had allotted portions of that land to the families of Israel; and He expected them to keep their inheritance as a sacred trust from Him. Naboth understood this and stood firm in his obedience to God's commands—even to the point of refusing the king!

Yet Naboth suffered for his obedience and paid the ultimate price for his faithfulness—he and all his sons with him. There was no "happy ending" to his story, for at Jezebel's instigation he was falsely accused of blasphemy against God and king and stoned to death outside the city walls. This was the grossest of injustices, yet it was Naboth's fate when he obeyed the Word of God. But we must remember this is not the true end to his story, which will unfold for us when we meet the Lord in eternity. At that time, Naboth will receive a great reward for his faithfulness, as will all who suffer injustice for obedience to God.

The Lord *does* permit His servants to suffer for being faithful to Him. After all, Jesus Himself suffered the grossest injustice of all men when He died for living a sinless life. Jesus warned us of the potential for suffering: "If the world hates you, you know that it hated Me before it hated you. If you were of the world, the world would love its own. Yet because you are not of the world, but I chose you out of the world, therefore the world hates you. Remember the word that I said to you, 'A servant is not greater than his master.' If they persecuted Me, they will also persecute you" (John 15:18–20).

When we disobey God, we sell out our soul to sin. Ahab wanted Naboth's vineyard, but Naboth wouldn't sell. Ahab bartered and pleaded, but Naboth stood firm. Ahab pouted, but Naboth ignored him. So the mighty king of Israel, who had just won an amazing military victory against a world superpower, stomped off to his bedroom to sulk. He threw himself on his bed, turned his face to the wall, and pettishly refused to eat any food. Ahab's temper tantrum led to his wife's intervention, and her plan led to the death of Naboth.

When Elijah later confronted Ahab, he told the king that he had sold himself to do evil (see 1 Kings 21:20). In this case, Ahab had murdered in exchange for a vineyard. Previously, he had ignored the Lord's command in exchange for a bribe—the return of the cities that Ben-Hadad I of Syria had taken from his father, Omri. Ahab had faced a choice in each case: obey God, or forfeit his loyalty to fulfill his sinful desires. The Lord described both of these sins as a form of selling out.

When people sin, they are basically saying there is something they desire more than obedience to God. They are saying that a certain pleasure will bring more joy than the joy that comes from obedience. Sin is the selling out of our soul. In Ahab's case, he sold out his soul for a vineyard that he couldn't rightfully possess. He desired sin, and so he sold himself to serve it. This is what it means to be a slave to sin. When we sell our loyalty to God in exchange for sin, we become a servant to sin and an enemy to God.

REFLECTING ON THE TEXT

5) How did Jezebel gain such power and influence in Israel? How might things have been different if Ahab had not married her?

_____

_____

_____

_____

6) What did the Lord mean when He said that Ahab had sold himself (see 1 Kings 21:20)? In what sense had he done this? What led him to it? What resulted from it?

_____

_____

_____

_____

7) In what ways is coveting the same as idol worship? How did Ahab's idolatry lead him to covet his neighbor's land? How did idolatry lead him to murder?

_____

_____

_____

_____

8) How is contentment different from happiness? How does a person gain contentment? According to Philippians 4:11–13, how did Paul gain contentment?

_____

_____

_____

_____

PERSONAL RESPONSE

9) Are there any idols in your life? Are you presently coveting something (or someone) that you don't possess? How will you root out this sin?

_____

_____

_____

_____

10) What are some of the blessings that God has provided in your life?
List them below, and then spend some time thanking Him for them.
Repeat this each day for the coming week, and ask God to continue
to teach you contentment.

_____

_____

_____

_____

11

THE DEATH OF KING AHAB

1 Kings 22:1–40

DRAWING NEAR

Why is it so hard at times for people to hear the truth? Why it is easier to believe in a lie—even if we know that we are deluding ourselves in the process?

_____

_____

_____

THE CONTEXT

The book of 1 Kings is filled with the stories of numerous kings and various prophets, but one theme runs throughout the narrative: the kings of Israel rejected the Word of God, while the prophets of God spoke the truth to them boldly. In every case, those who rejected God's truth came to destruction, while the words of the prophets always proved true. In this study, we will finally see the words of Elijah and others come to reality in the life of Ahab, and we will see God's hand of judgment come down on that wicked king.

We will also meet Jehoshaphat, a king of Judah who actually feared the Lord and sought to do His will. We will find him, of all places, in the court of

Ahab, as the two kings—polar opposites in their approach to God's Word—make plans to go into war together. One might well ask what Jehoshaphat was doing there in the first place, but the answer is another theme that has run throughout these studies: Jehoshaphat had allied himself with the wicked family of Ahab through an ungodly marriage. The results of this unequal yoking were consistent with all the others we've seen in the book of 1 Kings.

In this study, we will also see how the ungodly hate the truth and the lengths to which they will go to replace it with lies—lies that make them happy, even when they know they're lies. This is the inevitable result for anyone who rejects the Word of God. It is a truly wise person who remains faithful to God's Word.

KEYS TO THE TEXT

Read 1 Kings 22:1–40, noting the key words and phrases indicated below.

MAKING PLANS FOR WAR: Jehoshaphat, the king of Judah, joins Ahab in Israel, and the two consider making war against Syria once again.

22:1. THREE YEARS PASSED: Israel had peace for three years following the two years of war with Syria. During this time, Ben-Hadad II, Ahab, and ten other kings formed a coalition to repel an Assyrian invasion. Although Assyria would claim victory, later events reveal they were stopped from further advance southward at that time. With the Assyrian threat neutralized, Ahab turned his attention to the unfinished conflict with Syria.

2. JEHOSHAPHAT: The son of Asa and the fourth king of Judah. His son Jehoram had married Ahab's daughter Athaliah, an alliance that would prove harmful for Jehoshaphat and calamitous for Jehoram. Jehoshaphat felt compelled by this relationship to associate himself with Ahab, while Ahab's daughter eventually led Jehoram into the idolatrous ways of Israel.

3. RAMOTH IN GILEAD: Ramoth was a Levitical city located east of the Jordan River in Gilead. During Solomon's time, it served as a key administrative center in the kingdom of Israel. Ben-Hadad II had promised to return to Ahab this city and all the others that Syria had taken away, but he evidently had not fulfilled that promise.

SEEKING GOD'S WILL: Jehoshaphat does not want to make plans without first asking what the Lord desires. However, this raises a problem, because only one king serves the Lord.

5. PLEASE INQUIRE FOR THE WORD OF THE LORD: Jehoshaphat set an example to Ahab by insisting they seek the Lord's counsel before going into battle. It is likely that Ahab would have charged forward without God's guidance if Jehoshaphat had not insisted.

6. GATHERED THE PROPHETS TOGETHER: These were not true prophets of the Lord, but false prophets whom Ahab had gathered around him. They worshiped the golden calves set up by Jeroboam, so their words were obviously not from God. They refused to begin their prophecies with the authoritative "thus says the LORD" and did not even use the covenant name *Yahweh* for the one true God of Israel.

7. A PROPHET OF THE LORD: Jehoshaphat quickly recognized these men were not true prophets and insisted they consult a man whose words would be from God.

8. THERE IS STILL ONE MAN, MICAIAH . . . BUT I HATE HIM: Micaiah's name means "who is like the LORD?" One can almost picture Ahab stamping his foot and pouting as he told Jehoshaphat about this man. This prophet had the courage to speak the truth to Ahab, but the king of Israel was less interested in hearing the truth than in hearing words that pleased him.

LET NOT THE KING SAY SUCH THINGS: Jehoshaphat rebuked Ahab for placing his own desires above the true word of God spoken through His prophet. The true prophet of God will speak God's Word regardless of whether it brings a message of encouragement or judgment, while the false prophet of the world will design his message to please his hearers. Jesus would later warn His disciples, "Beware of false prophets, who come to you in sheep's clothing, but inwardly they are ravenous wolves. You will know them by their fruit" (Matthew 7:15–16).

9. BRING MICAIAH THE SON OF IMLAH QUICKLY: It appears that Ahab was growing impatient at this point. He certainly didn't want to be confronted by Micaiah, for fear the prophet would say things that displeased him. Yet he also wanted to do what Jehoshaphat asked, because he wanted to go into battle with him. He had already convinced himself that his plan was right, and was impatient to get on with it. Ahab was consistently both immature and impetuous.

THE FALSE PROPHETS SPEAK: As Jehoshaphat and Ahab wait for Micaiah's arrival, the 400 false prophets make their own false predictions about the outcome of the battle.

10. AT A THRESHING FLOOR: Threshing floors were hard-packed spaces in the open air where wheat and other grains were beaten out. These areas were common sites for meetings of royal courts at the time, but threshing is also used in Scripture to speak of God's winnowing process, in which He separates the wheat from the chaff, the godly from the fleshly. It was an appropriate setting for this important meeting, as God was about to separate the truth from the lies.

11. ZEDEKIAH . . . HAD MADE HORNS OF IRON FOR HIMSELF: Zedekiah was evidently the spokesman for the 400 false prophets. He used visual aids in his presentation to the kings, which undoubtedly made his message seem more convincing and powerful. But the Lord's truth is frequently couched in humble terms, while the messages of the world are often far more entertaining and compelling to the flesh.

THUS SAYS THE LORD: By speaking these words, Zedekiah was claiming his message was a direct revelation from God. Anyone who made this claim falsely was to be put to death, and the test was whether or not the prophesied events came to pass (see Deuteronomy 18:20–22).

12. ALL THE PROPHETS PROPHESIED SO: The false prophets were unanimous in their encouragement. Ahab had surrounded himself with people who would tell him exactly what he wanted to hear, and they did not disappoint him in this situation. Nothing could ruin Ahab's plan but for a real prophet to show up and contradict the false prophecies.

GOD'S PROPHET SPEAKS: Micaiah, the true prophet of the Lord, now arrives on the scene. Just as Ahab predicted, Micaiah's words are not what the king of Israel wants to hear.

13. NOW LISTEN: One can picture this messenger whispering in Micaiah's ear, offering him some worldly wisdom. "Don't rock the boat," he essentially said. "Everyone else is in agreement on this, so do yourself a favor—do *everyone* a favor—and just go along with it."

14. THAT I WILL SPEAK: The prophet of God always speaks the truth, whether or not it will sit comfortably with those who hear it.

15. GO AND PROSPER: Micaiah was not delivering the Lord's message at this point but using sarcasm to underscore the fact that Ahab's prophets were only saying what he wanted to hear.

16. TELL ME NOTHING BUT THE TRUTH: Ahab recognized Micaiah's sarcasm and understood he was not speaking the word of the Lord. This underscores the fact that, in Ahab's heart, he knew his own "wise men" were false prophets.

17. SHEEP THAT HAVE NO SHEPHERD: The image of the king as a shepherd and his people as the sheep was a familiar one to the Israelites. Micaiah's point was that Israel's "shepherd," King Ahab, would soon be killed and his army scattered.

19. HEAR THE WORD OF THE LORD: Micaiah was claiming that his words were a direct revelation from God, just as Zedekiah had claimed. However, the two prophecies were mutually exclusive, so the final test would be to see which one came true. Micaiah's statement that he "saw the LORD" indicates he received this prophecy through a vision. Other prophets would also record such visions, including Isaiah (see Isaiah 6) and the apostle John (see Revelation 1:9; 4:1).

A LYING SPIRIT: Micaiah now reveals that the Lord had sent an evil spirit to influence Ahab's false prophets so they would urge the king of Israel to go into battle.

20. WHO WILL PERSUADE AHAB: Many prophetic visions describe conversations between God and angelic beings within His heavenly court. Job, for example, described such a conversation involving Satan, who was permitted to test him (see Job 1–2).

22. A LYING SPIRIT: Good angels do not lie, so we know the being who spoke these words was a demonic spirit. Like the devil himself, this spirit was subject to the authority and power of God and had to come and go from His presence at His command. The Lord uses all things—even the wickedness of Satan—to further His own plans, and nothing can thwart His sovereignty. At the same time, those who disobey God's Word will be accountable for their disobedience, just as Ahab was about to be brought to account for his wickedness.

23. THE LORD HAS PUT A LYING SPIRIT: The Lord "put" the lying spirit in the mouths of the false prophets in the sense that He permitted demons to mislead them. God is not the author of evil, however, and He never lies—nor does He ever encourage His creatures to speak lies. This is just an example of how God permits evil and uses it to further His own plans—though He does not condone the evil behavior in the process.

24. STRUCK MICAIAH ON THE CHEEK: This was a rebuke from the leader of the false prophets for the perceived insolence of Micaiah and his claim to truly speak for God. Zedekiah followed this by a sarcastic question in which he asked if the prophet could tell which direction the spirit of the Lord had gone from him. The world's prophets often go beyond just ignoring the Word of God in this way—they actually hate it and lash out against those who preach it. Jesus would later receive similar treatment from the chief priests (see Mark 14:65).

27. PUT THIS FELLOW IN PRISON: Here again, we see that the Lord will permit His servants to suffer for His Word—even as His Son, Jesus, suffered on the cross. Ahab's foolishness was on clear display here. He mistakenly thought that if he jailed the prophet, God would let him live. Simply put, Ahab was trying to manipulate the Lord.

28. IF YOU EVER RETURN IN PEACE . . . TAKE HEED: Micaiah once again reiterated the test for all prophets. If just one prophecy does not come to pass or is in contradiction to the written Word of God, that person is not speaking God's message.

AHAB'S LAST STAND: Ahab disregards the Lord's dire warnings and goes off to battle. He thinks he can outsmart God by disguising himself, but he will be proven wrong.

30. I WILL DISGUISE MYSELF: Kings generally wore royal robes into battle so their army would see them leading the charge. These robes made them stand out in the heat of battle, so they were easy targets for the enemy. Ahab's choice to disguise himself and not wear these robes suggests he feared Micaiah's prophecy would come to pass.

31. THE KING OF SYRIA: This was Ben-Hadad II, whom Ahab had allowed to live after Israel had defeated the Syrian army. The Lord had prophesied that Ahab would give his life in exchange for Ben-Hadad II (see 1 Kings 20:42), and here the divine prediction was fulfilled.

32. JEHOSHAPHAT CRIED OUT: According to 2 Chronicles 18:31, this was a prayer for the Lord's deliverance. Jehoshaphat's cry revealed to the Syrians that he was not Ahab.

34. A CERTAIN MAN DREW A BOW AT RANDOM: Ahab thought he could outsmart the sovereign God by disguising himself, but the Lord's purposes can never be thwarted. In this case, God used an unnamed soldier who shot an arrow at random, and He guided that arrow into a small groove between the breastplate and flexible scale armor that covered Ahab's lower abdomen and thighs. This would be perceived by the world as a random event, a striking coincidence, but it was actually God's deliberate hand intervening to work a miracle.

35. THE KING WAS PROPPED UP IN HIS CHARIOT: Ahab was mortally wounded in the stomach and asked his driver to take him out of the battle. To keep up the morale of the army of Israel—who would have fled if they had seen their king fall—Ahab's servants propped him up to make it appear as though he were still fighting. The king died in the evening.

38. THE DOGS LICKED UP HIS BLOOD WHILE THE HARLOTS BATHED: This was just what Elijah had prophesied (see 1 Kings 21:19). Ahab had prostituted himself and the entire nation of Israel with foreign gods, so it was fitting that he should end his life in company with harlots.

UNLEASHING THE TEXT

1) Why did Jehoshaphat agree to go into battle with Ahab? In what ways did this decision show a lack of wisdom on his part?

_____

_____

_____

2) How did Ahab's marriage to Jezebel affect his leadership? How did the marriage of Jehoshaphat's son to Ahab's daughter affect his leadership?

_____

_____

_____

3) Why did Ahab surround himself with false prophets? Why did he heed their advice, even when he knew it was wrong? How do people do the same thing today?

_____

_____

_____

4) Why did Ahab disguise himself when he went into battle? What did he think he would gain? What did this reveal about his understanding of God's truth?

_____

_____

_____

EXPLORING THE MEANING

Speak the truth, especially in the face of opposition. Ahab hated Micaiah because he always said things that upset him. When everyone else was predicting his success for Ahab, Micaiah would come along and predict doom and gloom. What made it worse was that Micaiah was always right, because he was speaking God's message. It wasn't so much that Ahab hated Micaiah personally, but more that he hated God's Word.

Micaiah and Elijah had two things in common: they were both hated by Ahab and they both spoke God's truth with boldness. They stood in stark contrast to a world around them that only wanted to hear pleasant words—but these pleasant words only led Ahab to his destruction. The reality is that sometimes the truth is not pleasant to hear, but it is always necessary for us to be given it. In the same way, though God's Word may contain things that we find uncomfortable, it is a sword that still must be wielded.

After all, what good is it to have a sharp sword during combat if we refuse to use it? As Christians we must remember that we are living in a battle zone, and the war for our souls is raging all around us. As Paul exhorted Timothy, "I charge you therefore before God and the Lord Jesus Christ, who will judge the living and the dead at His appearing and His kingdom: Preach the word! Be ready in season and out of season. Convince, rebuke, exhort, with all longsuffering and teaching" (2 Timothy 4:1–2). We must use God's sword with love—but use it!

Test the teachings of men against the truths of Scripture. Ahab surrounded himself with hundreds of false prophets whom he could count on to say the things he wanted to hear. These men made no attempt to ask God for wisdom, yet they spoke authoritatively in God's name and claimed their words were true. In fact, the Lord had actually permitted a lying spirit—the devil himself—to lead these men into speaking lies.

The world is filled with men and women who claim to know truth but actually speak lies. Many of these false prophets are convincing, and their followers may be legion—but this does not make their words true. Christians are called on to test every teaching and every doctrine against the Scriptures to determine what is true and what is false. Any teacher, prophet, or leader who makes any claims that contradict the Bible should be considered a false prophet.

As John warned in one of his letters, "Do not believe every spirit, but test the spirits, whether they are of God; because many false prophets have gone out into the world. By this you know the Spirit of God: Every spirit that confesses that Jesus Christ has come in the flesh is of God, and every spirit that does not confess that Jesus Christ has come in the flesh is not of God. And this is the spirit of the Antichrist, which you have heard was coming, and is now already in the world" (1 John 4:1–3). This should be the pattern for all Christians: test all teachings against the Bible and consider anything that contradicts God's Word to be false.

God cannot be fooled. Micaiah clearly told Ahab that he would die in the battle against Syria, but instead of repenting and asking God for forgiveness, Ahab tried to manipulate the Lord. Ahab had the prophet jailed and said he was not to be released until the king returned from battle—as if the Lord would be forced to spare Ahab so Micaiah could be freed!

Ahab then disguised himself as he went to battle. It appears that Ahab thought God could not kill him if God could not find him. Obviously, the Lord saw through the disguise, and when the archer shot Ahab "at random," the king's attempt to avoid judgment for his sin failed. Ahab learned what should have been an obvious lesson: God's judgment cannot be avoided because God cannot be fooled.

Paul describes this truth in his letter to the Galatians: "Do not be deceived, God is not mocked; for whatever a man sows, this he will also reap" (Galatians 6:7). People often think they will somehow be able to outwit God and avoid His judgment, but the truth is that such trickery is impossible. However, God *did* provide a way for us to escape the eternal consequences of judgment through the sacrifice of Jesus on the cross. If we believe that Jesus is the Son of God, that His death was in payment for our sins, and that God raised Him from the grave, we will be spared the judgment of God. The Lord cannot be tricked or fooled, and the only escape from judgment is through belief in the gospel.

REFLECTING ON THE TEXT

5) Why did God send a lying spirit into the false prophets? What does this reveal about God's sovereignty? What does it reveal about the way He operates in our world?

_____

_____

_____

6) In Old Testament times, how did the people know whether a prophet was truly speaking God's Word or not? How do we know today?

_____

_____

_____

7) In what ways do people in our culture choose to heed the words of false prophets? Why do people deliberately reject God's truth in favor of such false prophets?

_____

_____

_____

_____

8) When have you boldly spoken the truth, even though it was unpopular? What was the result? When have you not spoken the truth out of fear? What was the result?

_____

_____

_____

_____

PERSONAL RESPONSE

9) Do you test every teaching by comparing it to the Bible? Do you read the Bible on a daily basis? If not, make a plan to begin reading one chapter each day for the coming week.

_____

_____

_____

10) In what ways have you seen others attempting to avoid God's judgment? In your own life, how does the knowledge that Jesus paid the penalty for your sin affect the way you view the judgment of God?

_____

_____

_____

_____

12

REVIEWING KEY PRINCIPLES

DRAWING NEAR

As you look back at each of the studies in 1 Kings 12–22, what is the one thing that stood out to you the most? What is one new perspective you have learned?

_____

_____

_____

THE CONTEXT

During the last eleven studies, you have witnessed the united kingdom of Israel divide into two parts, met some of the kings who rose up to rule these kingdoms, and—with a few notable exceptions—watched as they led their people into idolatry. For the most part, from Solomon onward, most of those kings refused to obey the Word of God, choosing instead to live as they pleased and worship whatever god they chose. We have also met prophets of God such as Elijah, who confronted those kings and boldly spoke the truth at great cost to themselves.

One theme has remained constant throughout these studies: _God is faithful, and those who obey Him will grow in faithfulness as well._ Every king of Israel, and many of Judah, proved themselves to be unfaithful not only to the nation they were supposed to be shepherding but also to God Himself. In contrast, God's prophets were faithful both to God and to His people, even though they were in danger of losing life or liberty. In the same way, when we are faithful to God's Word, we will always discover that He is faithful to us.

Here are a few of the major principles we have found during our study. There are many more we don't have room to reiterate, so take some time to review the earlier studies—or, better still, to meditate on the Scripture that we have covered. As you do, ask the Holy Spirit to give you wisdom and insight into His Word. He will not refuse.

EXPLORING THE MEANING

Divine sovereignty does not nullify human responsibility. The Lord prophesied that He would tear the kingdom away from Solomon's son and divide the nation of Israel into two separate kingdoms. He used the foolish decisions of Rehoboam and the rebellious spirit of Israel to accomplish this purpose—yet this did not exonerate Rehoboam from culpability for his foolishness or the people of Israel for their sin. God is indeed sovereign over all the affairs of humankind, but this does not mean He will not judge individuals for their actions.

Jesus again provides the perfect example of this principle. It was God's plan from the foundation of the world that His perfect Son should offer Himself as a sacrifice to redeem sinful men, and God used the evil deeds of those who rejected Christ to accomplish that plan. Yet this did not exonerate those who crucified Christ for their deeds. In the same way, it does not exonerate anyone who rejects Jesus as the only way to salvation and peace with God.

The good news is that God uses all things to further His purposes in our lives. When we live in obedience to His Word, we can rest in the assurance that God is completely sovereign over all the events and circumstances that come our way, and He will turn all things to His glory and our blessing. "All things work together for good to those who love God, to those who are the called according to His purpose" (Romans 8:28).

Syncretism is a form of idolatry. Syncretism is the act of mixing together elements from different religions to create a sort of hybrid religious system. The process can refer to intermingling diverse religious practices, or it can refer to those who attempt to reconcile opposing viewpoints. Jeroboam committed the sin of syncretism when he attempted to mingle pagan idolatry with God's commanded worship. It is easy to see the idolatry of Jeroboam's acts, as he literally created two golden calves for the people to worship.

But syncretism is still idolatry even when it doesn't involve golden calves. The basic motivation behind syncretism is rebellion against God's Word. Individuals decide they want to worship God in their own way and reject certain aspects of Scripture in favor of their own ideas. This is the idolatry of self—making oneself to be equal with God and pushing the Lord into the background, just as Jeroboam did. The world continually encourages syncretism for the simple reason that it hates the teachings of Christ and does everything in its power to move believers away from God's Word. Many use the excuse that the gospel must be made "relevant" to our culture to ignore scriptural principles and add in principles that are not scriptural.

Such attempts to mix the teachings of the world with the doctrines of God's Word are syncretistic. The Bible is the final authority on how to approach God, and we do not have the privilege of rewriting Scripture to fit our own desires or to fit into the culture of the world around us. When cultural teachings and practices go against the teachings of the Bible, we are called to choose between the two—but not to attempt some compromise incorporating elements of both. We are called to choose once and for all to serve God, and to serve Him in His way, not in our own way. Anything else is idolatry.

The Lord is in control, even when His people are foolish. Even during Solomon's life the Lord had declared that the unified nation of Israel would be split into two. God had told Jeroboam he would rule ten of the tribes, which revealed the consequences of Solomon's sin. The Lord would not allow His people to prosper and be blessed while they were pursuing other gods.

However, notice the way in which the Lord allowed the division to happen. Rehoboam was foolish and rejected the wise counsel of his father's advisors while listening to the brash counsel of his friends. Meanwhile, Jeroboam was establishing calves as centers of worship, marking a permanent break between Israel and Judah. Rehoboam's foolishness and Jeroboam's idolatry were both sinful, but they were also the means by which the Lord fulfilled His prophecy that the kingdom would be divided.

It is important for us to understand that God is in control even when the world seems out of control. In fact, God often uses sin and its effects to bring about His perfect plan. No event in Scripture illustrates this truth as well as the betrayal and crucifixion of Jesus. Pilate was judged for betraying the Prince of Life, but Jesus said that Pilate only had the power to do what God had ordained (see John 19:11). Similarly, Judas was judged for betraying Jesus, but this sinful act of betrayal was what led to the death of Christ and the consummation of God's plan of salvation. Of course, this never excuses sin, but it does assure us that God is in charge of all things, and that all things are working for His glory (see Romans 11:36).

The godly leader leads by example. During the early years of King Asa's reign, he was a good leader for God's people because he ruled by example more than by command. It is true that he commanded the people of Judah to seek the Lord and to obey His precepts, but he first set the example by doing it himself. He turned away from the idolatry of his predecessors and removed the sites where such pagan practices took place. When he was faced with an overwhelming enemy during those early years, he turned to the Lord for protection rather than trusting in the power of his army or in alliances with others.

David was another king who led by example rather than by command. David's heart was always turned toward the Lord, and he strove throughout his life to be faithful to God's Word. When he did fall into sin, he was quick to repent when a prophet of God confronted him—which was contrary to Asa's response in his later years. Under David, the people could look to their king for an example of how to lead a godly life. This was exactly what God intended.

The New Testament teaches the same principle for all those who are in authority. Husbands are called to love their wives as Christ loved the church (see Ephesians 5:25). Elders are called to lead their flock by living as Jesus lived (see 1 Timothy 3:1–7). Older men and women are called to live godly lives so that those who are younger might learn by their examples (see Titus 2:1–5). In fact, each of us is called to live out the principles of Scripture, regardless of our situations in life, so that we might be a living testimony to the world around us of what it means to be a follower of Christ.

Sin is never trivial. Jeroboam instituted idolatry in Israel, attempting to mix it together with the nation's worship of God. This was a grievous sin for which the Lord judged him, yet Ahab acted "as though it had been a trivial thing" (1 Kings 16:31). By the time Ahab became king, the nation had been embracing Jeroboam's sinful practices for some fifty years, and the people had probably grown so accustomed to it that it seemed normal. This attitude of shrugging off sin led Ahab into even greater wickedness, and eventually it brought about the downfall of all Israel.

Sin is never trivial in God's eyes, but when we as believers in Christ ignore it or indulge in it, we can become inured to it. In fact, we can grow so accustomed to wickedness that we cease to be bothered by it—and even accept it as normal behavior in the world around us. The danger of this nonchalance is that if we don't take sin seriously, we can begin to slide into embracing it ourselves.

God hates sin, and He calls His people to hate it as He does. It is easy to become complacent about disobedience, which is why we must always guard against becoming comfortable with sin by spending time in God's Word and in regular fellowship with other believers. As James warns us, "Friendship with the world is enmity with God. Whoever therefore wants to be a friend of the world makes himself an enemy of God. . . . Draw near to God and He will draw near to you. Cleanse your hands, you sinners; and purify your hearts, you double-minded" (James 4:4, 8).

Be bold to speak God's truth, even when you are the only one. Imagine how Elijah must have felt when he stood on Mount Carmel all by himself, facing 850 hostile pagan priests, a powerful king who was looking for an excuse to execute him, and a crowd of Israelites who were indifferent at best to his fate. The entire nation had at least adulterated their worship practices with paganism, and the most powerful and influential in the land had embraced Baal outright. What's more, the priests of Baal had official endorsement from the queen herself. They were the appointed leaders of the official state religion, and arguing against them was just not done.

Yet Elijah stood on the mountainside and did just this—he argued loudly and urgently against the false teachings of the world around him, even though nobody came up and stood beside him. Christians may find themselves in similar situations, especially as the world continues to move more openly into all manner of heathenism. It can be intimidating to take a stand against the false doctrines of the world today, but God calls us to do so nonetheless.

It is important to remember two points in this regard. First, Elijah may have felt alone, but in fact the Lord had preserved a remnant in Israel of those who were faithful to Him. Second, Elijah would not have been alone even if he *had* been the last faithful man in Israel—for he stood in the presence of the

Almighty. The anger of those around him was ultimately not directed at him but at God, and God would never abandon His devoted prophet. When we remember that we serve an omnipotent God who is always holding us in His hand, we will be encouraged to stand up boldly—even if we stand alone.

When we disobey God, we sell out our soul to sin. Ahab wanted Naboth's vineyard, but Naboth wouldn't sell. Ahab bartered and pleaded, but Naboth stood firm. Ahab pouted, but Naboth ignored him. So the mighty king of Israel, who had just won an amazing military victory against a world superpower, stomped off to his bedroom to sulk. He threw himself on his bed, turned his face to the wall, and pettishly refused to eat any food. Ahab's temper tantrum led to his wife's intervention, and her plan led to the death of Naboth.

When Elijah later confronted Ahab, he told the king that he had sold himself to do evil (see 1 Kings 21:20). In this case, Ahab had murdered in exchange for a vineyard. Previously, he had ignored the Lord's command in exchange for a bribe—the return of the cities that Ben-Hadad I of Syria had taken from his father, Omri. Ahab had faced a choice in each case: obey God, or forfeit his loyalty to fulfill his sinful desires. The Lord described both of these sins as a form of selling out.

When people sin, they are basically saying there is something they desire more than obedience to God. They are saying that a certain pleasure will bring more joy than the joy that comes from obedience. Sin is the selling out of our soul. In Ahab's case, he sold out his soul for a vineyard that he couldn't rightfully possess. He desired sin, and so he sold himself to serve it. This is what it means to be a slave to sin. When we sell our loyalty to God in exchange for sin, we become a servant to sin and an enemy to God.

Test the teachings of men against the truths of Scripture. Ahab surrounded himself with hundreds of false prophets whom he could count on to say the things he wanted to hear. These men made no attempt to ask God for wisdom, yet they spoke authoritatively in God's name and claimed their words were true. In fact, the Lord had actually permitted a lying spirit—the devil himself—to lead these men into speaking lies.

The world is filled with men and women who claim to know truth but actually speak lies. Many of these false prophets are convincing, and their followers may be legion—but this does not make their words true. Christians are called on to test every teaching and every doctrine against the Scriptures to determine what is true and what is false. Any teacher, prophet, or leader who makes any claims that contradict the Bible should be considered a false prophet.

As John warned in one of his letters, "Do not believe every spirit, but test the spirits, whether they are of God; because many false prophets have gone out into the world. By this you know the Spirit of God: Every spirit that confesses that Jesus Christ has come in the flesh is of God, and every spirit that does not confess that Jesus Christ has come in the flesh is not of God. And this is the spirit of the Antichrist, which you have heard was coming, and is now already in the world" (1 John 4:1–3). This should be the pattern for all Christians: test all teachings against the Bible and consider anything that contradicts God's Word to be false.

Unleashing the Text

1) Which of the concepts or principles in this study have you found to be the most encouraging? Why?

_____

_____

_____

_____

2) Which of the concepts or principles have you found most challenging? Why?

_____

_____

_____

_____

3) What aspects of "walking with God" are you already doing in your life? Which areas need strengthening?

_____

_____

_____

_____

4) To which of the characters that we've studied have you most been able to relate? How might you emulate that person in your own life?

_____

_____

_____

_____

PERSONAL RESPONSE

5) Have you taken a definite stand for Jesus Christ? Have you accepted His free gift of salvation? If not, what is preventing you from doing so?

_____

_____

_____

_____

_____

6) What areas of your life have been most convicted during this study? What exact things will you do to address these convictions? Be specific.

_____

_____

_____

7) What have you learned about the character of God during this study? How has this insight affected your worship or prayer life?

_____

_____

_____

_____

8) What are some specific things you want to see God do in your life in the coming month? What are some things you intend to change in your own life during that time? (Return to this list in one month and hold yourself accountable to fulfill these things.)

_____

_____

_____

If you would like to continue in your study of the Old Testament, read the next title in this series: _2 Kings: The Fall of Judah and Israel._

ALSO AVAILABLE

JOHN MACARTHUR

EXODUS & NUMBERS

THE EXODUS FROM EGYPT

I n this study, John MacArthur guides readers through an in-depth look at the historical period beginning with God's calling of Moses, continuing through the giving of the Ten Commandments, and concluding with the Israelites' preparations to enter the Promised Land. This study includes close-up examinations of Aaron, Caleb, Joshua, Balaam and Balak, as well as careful considerations of doctrinal themes such as "Complaints and Rebellion" and "Following God's Law."

The MacArthur Bible Studies provide intriguing examinations of the whole of Scripture. Each guide incorporates extensive commentary, detailed observations on overriding themes, and probing questions to help you study the Word of God with guidance from John MacArthur.

ALSO AVAILABLE

In this study, John MacArthur guides readers through an in-depth look at the Israelites' conquest of the Promised Land, beginning with the miraculous parting of the Jordan River, continuing through the victories and setbacks as the people settled into Canaan, and concluding with the time of the judges. Studies include close-up examinations of Rahab, Ruth, and Samson, as well as careful considerations of doctrinal themes such as "The Sin of Achan" and the role of "The Kinsman Redeemer."

The MacArthur Bible Studies provide intriguing examinations of the whole of Scripture. Each guide incorporates extensive commentary, detailed observations on overriding themes, and probing questions to help you study the Word of God with guidance from John MacArthur.

ALSO AVAILABLE

In this study, John MacArthur guides readers through an in-depth look at this historical period beginning with the miraculous birth of Samuel, continuing through Saul's crowning as Israel's first king, and concluding with his tragic death. Studies include close-up examinations of Hannah, Eli, Saul, David, and Jonathan, as well as careful considerations of doctrinal themes such as "Slaying a Giant" and "Respecting God's Anointed."

The MacArthur Bible Studies provide intriguing examinations of the whole of Scripture. Each guide incorporates extensive commentary, detailed observations on overriding themes, and probing questions to help you study the Word of God with guidance from John MacArthur.

ALSO AVAILABLE

In this study, John MacArthur guides readers through an in-depth look at the historical period beginning with David's struggle to establish his throne, continuing through his sin and repentance, and concluding with the tragic rebellion of his son Absalom. Studies include close-up examinations of Joab, Amnon, Tamar, Absalom, and others, as well as careful considerations of doctrinal themes such as "Obedience and Blessing" and being a "Man After God's Own Heart."

The MacArthur Bible Studies provide intriguing examinations of the whole of Scripture. Each guide incorporates extensive commentary, detailed observations on overriding themes, and probing questions to help you study the Word of God with guidance from John MacArthur.